Of Houses & Time

Of Houses & Time

PERSONAL HISTORIES OF AMERICA'S
NATIONAL TRUST PROPERTIES

William Seale

HARRY N. ABRAMS, INC., PUBLISHERS
NEW YORK

IN ASSOCIATION WITH THE
NATIONAL TRUST FOR HISTORIC PRESERVATION

Page 2: The Shadows-on-the-Teche in the 1920s (Martin Photo, Shadows-on-the-Teche). Page 5: The hearth — center of many Wright houses — in the architect's Oak Park home and studio (Jon Miller, © Hedrich-Blessing). Page 6: The dining room of the Cooper-Molera Adobe restored to its late nineteenth-century appearance (David Livingston). Page 8: The entrance hall at Cliveden (Ping Amranand). Page 9: Decorative plasterwork in the hall of Oatlands, looking toward the portrait of William Corcoran Eustis (Ping Amranand). Pages 10–11: The Gothic castle Lyndhurst at sunset (Mick Hales). Pages 12–13: Filoli's garden pool with allées of yew trees and some of its floral splendors (© Alexander Vertikoff). Pages 14–15: Drayton Hall (Gordon Beall), Oatlands (Erik Kvalsvik), Lyndhurst (Jim Frank), Belle Grove (Ping Amranand), Brucemore (Bradley Photographics), Chesterwood (Robert Lautman), Filoli (© Alexander Vertikoff), Montpelier (Ping Amranand). Page 16: President Wilson's memorabilia and a portrait of Edith Wilson in the Woodrow Wilson House (Gordon Beall).

Project Manager for Abrams: Julia Moore

PRODUCED BY ARCHETYPE PRESS, INC., WASHINGTON, D.C.

Project Director: Diane Maddex

Art Directors: Marc Alain Meadows and Robert L. Wiser

Library of Congress Cataloging-in-Publication Data
Seale, William.
Of houses & time : personal histories of America's National
Trust properties / William Seale.
p.   cm.
Includes bibliographical references and index.
ISBN 0-8109-3671-2
1. Historic buildings — United States. 2. Dwellings — United States.
3. Architecture, Domestic — United States — History.
I. Title.
E159.S48 1992

973—dc20   92-4703 CIP

Text copyright © 1992 William Seale

Published in 1992 by Harry N. Abrams, Incorporated, New York
A Times Mirror Company

Printed and bound in Japan

Dedicated to Howard W. Smith, Jr.

❧

THIS BOOK WAS MADE POSSIBLE IN PART THROUGH A GENEROUS
GRANT IN MEMORY OF CHARLES HENRY WOODWARD

Colonial Empires 25

Within the walls of Drayton Hall, Cliveden, and Montpelier, colonial families decide whether to remain loyal to the king or join the colonies in revolt.

Children of the Revolution 49

The first generation of citizens expresses the new nation's high aspirations in its houses: Montpelier is enlarged by James Madison, and Belle Grove, Wood-lawn, and Oatlands arise as visions of others. Commodore Stephen Decatur builds a mansion in view of his next objective, the White House.

Age of Enterprise 85

While a Manhattan entrepreneur constructs a Hudson River castle, later named Lyndhurst, a Louisiana planter builds the Shadows beside Bayou Teche. In far-distant Monterey, Mexican California gains the Cooper-Molera Adobe and Casa Amesti, two houses made of earth and timber.

Houses Divided 115

The fires of the Civil War scorch in many ways: Cliveden is torn apart by family strife. The young master of Drayton Hall runs away to fight. The great Shenandoah Valley Campaign envelops Belle Grove. Oatlands, Woodlawn, the Shadows, Decatur House— all are affected.

Victorian Ambitions 131

The war irrevocably changes American life. The Chews at Cliveden regret it. Others celebrate its end by building Victorian wonders such as Brucemore. A rustic California hero becomes a polished diplomat at Decatur House. Lyndhurst sprouts new towers and a minaret on a fabulous greenhouse.

Art Turns the Century 155

Architect, sculptor, playwright—each makes his home his workplace: Frank Lloyd Wright in Oak Park, Daniel Chester French at Chesterwood, and Paul Kester at Woodlawn.

America Joins the World 177

A garden of dreams is planted at Filoli. Montpelier, Oatlands, and Belle Grove find new lives as country places. Woodrow Wilson moves to Embassy Row. Usonia takes form in Wright's Pope-Leighey House. Two romantics restore in California and Louisiana.

A Place for the Past 209

These houses have been occupied for long years, some for two centuries. Those who live in them begin to ask who will care for them when they no longer can.

Preface

More than 250 years of American history are reflected in the personal histories and houses described in this book. While you may know something about the houses already, only a few of the characters are widely known: James and Dolley Madison, Stephen Decatur, Woodrow Wilson, Frank Lloyd Wright, Martin Van Buren, sculptor Daniel Chester French, and, briefly, the movie star Randolph Scott. More numerous are the people you probably have never heard of: a pious Manhattan mayor who built a Gothic castle; proud southern planters of indigo, sugar, and sweet potatoes; *Californios,* married to foreigners, who owned empires in land along the Pacific; a shrewd Pennsylvania judge whose country house became a fort during the American Revolution; a widow on the Iowa prairie who absorbed her grief in the construction of a tall, sharp-gabled residence considered the best house between Chicago and San Francisco; and a hard-minded business-man who created a garden of dreams, then eventually let it close in around him as protection from the world. Famous or obscure, these characters, like practically all people, are revealed in the places in which they live.

Some of the characters—the text's main focus—were the actual builders of the houses, but more of them lived there in later years. As generations passed, various inhabitants became aware that they were living in "historic" places, and the most devoted undertook to preserve them. The preservation process can be consuming. One of the houses, for example, was patched and for more than a century was barely kept up, practically empty of furniture, but somehow the family, who lived elsewhere, could not let it go. It stands today as they kept it. Over the past forty years, the seventeen houses came by various routes under the ownership of the National Trust for Historic Preservation. The story in this book is of their lives until they became National Trust museum properties.

Considering the large scale of the subject, this is a short book. Houses record time in a special way, reflecting not only those who lived there but also the periods in which they lived. Yet old houses are in a sense always new, in that they have ongoing lives. I have not covered every generation in every house, nor have I given the houses equal space, as my approach is neither architectural nor that of a guidebook. The owners of the colonial house Cliveden in Philadelphia, for example, were such perfect—and, to me, useful—Victorian antiquarians that I linger with them in that period somewhat to the exclusion of others. I have taken care in nearly every case to include the builders and the subsequent tenants who best provide a broader glimpse of their sort of people in their times. Those who preserved the houses, when ruin might have swept them away, naturally attracted me, for their relationships with the houses often approached feelings between humans. The result, I hope, provides a certain perspective on Americans and their houses from colonial days to the mid-twentieth century.

All that the houses of this book really share is their function today as preserved places, under the National Trust. But people, of course, are more mobile than houses, and in composing the early chapters in particular I was often amazed at how the characters crossed paths over the face of a growing America. I do not claim this book to be a cross section of American life in any comprehensive sense at any time in history. That worthy if complex objective would be too great for the present volume, and to build a broad base it would require using some houses that no longer stand. I wanted buildings that I could study firsthand, ones with supporting written and visual documentation. The main subject here is, therefore, not American living but individuals and their houses. I was drawn first to the houses, then the characters. I found that for all of the expressions of wealth and privilege the pretty houses may imply at a distance, their stories are not as obvious up close. Houses can be deceptive—and they were often built to deceive. Around them are the mysteries always associated with human beings. To those within them the grass at times seemed greener beyond. Life behind most of these paneled doors seldom evaded the rough and tumble of human experience, and it was unlike life today mainly in the shift of context.

The American landscape is dotted with historic buildings. For many years their survival was perilous because the reuse of land so often precluded the reuse of the buildings that stood on it. An entire generation of public officials, architects, and builders was trained to destroy and replace. The mentality is still prevalent, only less so than before. We are learning that buildings, like mountains, waterfalls, and very old trees, define a place. They are the signs as well as the symbols of a culture. Ask any person whose town or country has been laid waste, for example, a Romanian or someone from Detroit. Who can imagine the Arizona desert without its natural wonder, the Grand Canyon? At the same time, who can picture the Egyptian desert in any way other than with the pyramids, those monuments to human imagination and labor? The importance of an old building may lie not necessarily in fine architecture or famous history. It may have neither; but alone or in a group of other buildings, it may give presence to a street or a town through the continuity of time it represents—

indeed, embodies—and is as much an inheritance common to us all as Old Faithful or Mount Hood.

For some time I had wanted to bring together a group of American houses in a narrative history from the eighteenth century to our own time. The question was, which houses, and how many? By finally taking these examples, I can say that the National Trust has assembled my houses for me. My interest in ways of living has remained, but the preservation issue gained increasing attraction, particularly in the context of a nation more accustomed to discarding than keeping. The houses here came to the National Trust under no grand master plan, but their admission as Trust properties was the culmination of long private struggles for survival. If only because of the sheer quantity of buildings in this country, preservation will always be first a private effort. Old buildings cannot all be museums. From a preservationist's point of view, the history of the houses in this book in a sense is the story of all old buildings that have survived the perils of long years.

Acknowledgments

My first thanks go to Diane Maddex of Archetype Press, Inc., editor of the book, for her valuable involvement in every aspect of the work.

Charles M. Harris advised me on research and conducted a lot of it himself. The details are more numerous and the human connections more intricate thanks to him.

Frank E. Sanchis III, vice president for Stewardship of Historic Properties of the National Trust, and Buckley C. Jeppson, director, The Preservation Press, were always encouraging. The Trust's involvement in the book was generously supported by Mrs. Charles Henry Woodward.

Carl A. Ruthstrom gave this book time and attention through various drafts. His labors are deeply appreciated.

No book about places so far-flung could have been written without the help of those on the scene. At Belle Grove I thank Michael Gore, executive director, and Carter Lively, curator. Sherry B. Jenkins of the Winchester–Frederick County Historical Society helped me with James Murray Mason's Selma nearby. Peggy Whitworth, executive director, and Laura Hoover, curator, at Brucemore provided critiques, directed me to sources, and supplied photographs. Malcolm S. Millard and Katherine Elkins Boyd at Casa Amesti helped with initial research there, while Jonathan Williams, supervising ranger at the Cooper-Molera Adobe, provided sources and was a careful reader of the book's sections on California.

Wanda Styka, curator at Chesterwood, did yeoman service not only in providing direction for research in manuscripts and photographs but also double-checked me on my Daniel Chester French facts and read galleys, and Paul W. Ivory, director, gave his support. Thanks also to Mr. and Mrs. Peter Van S Rice for their help with Chesterwood. Cliveden's staff furnished historical materials and kindly and usefully read drafts of the entire manuscript; there I thank Jennifer Esler, executive director, Nancy E. Richards, Elizabeth Laurent, and Sandra McKenzie Lloyd. Jennifer Anderson-Lawrence of the Winterthur Museum shared her excellent thesis on Cliveden and was helpful with research suggestions.

Vicki E. Sopher, director, Decatur House, reviewed the Decatur sections, as did Heather R. Palmer, collections specialist; Sarah Shaffer contributed advice and help with illustrations. I appreciate the assistance at Drayton Hall of Meggett B. Lavin, curator of education and research, and George N. McDaniel, director, as well as Tracy H. Hayes, Richmond Bowens, Robert E. L. Barker, and Tom Savage. Lynne Lewis, the National Trust archaeologist, read the Drayton parts of the manuscript. Samuel E. McIntosh was generous with his South Carolina historical sources and contacts. Anna Wells Rugledge shared with me her recollections of Charlotta Drayton, as did Charles Drayton.

Anne Taylor, director of Filoli, gave assistance early on, as did Sandra Wilcoxon, executive director of the Frank Lloyd Wright Home and Studio Foundation; Melanie Birk, public relations director, and Margaret Klinkow, research center director, assisted with photographs of Wright's home and studio. I thank Susanne Brendel Pandich, director, Lyndhurst, and Henry J. Duffy, curator, for help, encouragement, and illustrations. Professor Patrick Snayden shared his Lyndhurst research with me. Ann L. Miller, research coordinator at Montpelier, was helpful with research and as a reader; Dorrie Twitchell assisted me there at the outset, and I am grateful also to Christopher Scott, executive director, and Donna T. Bedwell, marketing director, for their help.

Kaye Napolitano, executive director of Oatlands, provided advice, and Melissa G. York, assistant director, and Lois Krumwiede, house manager, helped with illustrations. At the Shadows, Patricia L. Kahle, assistant director, shared extensive and ongoing research and reviewed galleys for accuracy. She and Director Shereen H. Minvielle helped me untangle the complexities of the Conrads and the Lewises. Michael T. Sheehan, director, and Frank Aucella, curator, Woodrow Wilson House, reviewed the manuscript and assisted with illustrations, as did Linda C. Goldstein, director, at Woodlawn; Anne H. Gorham provided guidance in researching Woodlawn and Frank Lloyd Wright's Pope-Leighey House. Tony Wrenn's work of long ago on Woodlawn is still a rich resource.

In addition to the above, I am grateful to Paul Gottlieb, president, Julia Moore, senior editor, and their colleagues at Harry N. Abrams, Inc., for shepherding the book to publication; Margaret Byrne Heimbold and John L. Heyl for their enthusiasm early on; Marc Alain Meadows and Robert L. Wiser of Archetype Press for their graphic design talents; Ann Townsend Payne for her secretarial assistance; and Lawrence Goldschmidt, George Siekkinen, Elizabeth Jones, Yvonne Cassells, Janet Walker, Jeff Roth, William Grenewald, and Pat Flowe for help at the National Trust. Morgan D. Delaney, M.D., greatly obliged me by reading the manuscript and giving his insights; Will Seale accompanied me on a field trip or two; John Henry Broocks Seale made many a fact-finding trip to the library; Mike and Kathy Merchant helped me with a crucial interview in California. And thanks last, but by no means least, to a very patient Lucinda S. Seale, who was there all along, in Virginia and Texas, while this book was written.

Colonial Empires

For the few who achieved personal wealth and public position in colonial America, a fine house was the crowning expression of status. Along the Atlantic seaboard John Drayton, a planter in South Carolina, and Benjamin Chew, a Philadelphia lawyer, built two such manifestations some seven hundred miles apart, the first a decade before the mid-eighteenth century and the other closer to the Revolution. The adjective *fine* being relative, an Englishman from the mother country might have described Chew's as merely a "good gentry house." Drayton Hall, the earlier of the two houses, was somewhat more.

During the years in which Drayton and Chew built their houses, Ambrose Madison established himself in simpler style on a large farm at the foot of the Blue Ridge Mountains in Virginia, at that time very far inland from the sea. His grandson James Madison was raised on this same farm, where a mansion also was eventually built; the grandson, of course, carried the Madison name higher than those of either Drayton or Chew.

The three colonial families were swept up in the powerful changes that came with the birth of the United States. Each had to make a momentous decision and

Opposite: Drayton Hall's land facade has double-stack porches, known as the portico, that once overlooked a long avenue of great oak trees extending to the public road. Wind-swept rooms opened off these porches, which themselves became open-air rooms during the warm seasons (Gordon Beall)

❧

Preceding pages: With its rich wood paneling and decorated plaster ceiling, the Ionic Drawing Room at Drayton Hall is one of colonial America's finest interiors. A member of the Drayton family replaced the original Georgian mantelpiece about 1803 with one in a more fashionable neoclassical style. This mantel was taken away by thieves in 1969 (Erik Kvalsvik)

stand by it, win or lose. Their houses were their homes before the American Revolution began. They served many generations that followed, and they still stand today, two of them much as they always were, and the third, Madison's home, greatly altered.

John Drayton, with a fortune in watery fields of rice and indigo, was the first rich man in his family line. Although he assembled most of his plantations on his own, he did have some land that was acquired by inheritance the generation before his. In a colonial culture not three-quarters of a century old, he—for all of his rough manner—qualified as a gentleman planter. While still in his early twenties in 1738, he purchased the 350-acre Ashley River tract on which Drayton Hall stands, outside Charleston, increasing it later to about sixteen hundred acres. This place was to be home. Few plantation lands in the Low Country of his time approximated in cost the £100-per-acre spent for the original part of this flat riverside sprawl of sandy earth.

Drayton always knew what he wanted. Hard willed, he dominated most of the people he encountered. The management system he created for his plantations made it possible for him to issue his commands through overseers and black labor captains. Paperwork was probably done by white office clerks. All were terrified of him. Drayton himself seems to have been no stranger to work, even work in the hot sun. Success was brought to him by the muscle and breath of others, including his African chattel and the English men and women he purchased for labor by indenture so many years at a time.

Drayton's earliest known forebears, English citizens of the island of Barbados, owned small plantations there—obscure people relative to him in his Ashley River splendor. In the late seventeenth century the Draytons joined the migration of small operators from the Caribbean, squeezed out by the great planters, and sought on the mainland better circumstances to satisfy a fever to grow. In South Carolina they and others from Barbados labored and connived to achieve political stability they had not known. Their coalition gained respect as the Goose Creek Party, named for the region where most of them settled. At least one term of indentured servitude can be found in John Drayton's family tree, and while his sons later acquired a crest, efforts by them and their own sons to link the name to aristocrats in England were never successful.

One wonders if Drayton ever concerned himself with his lineage, and one supposes ultimately not. Not a word of his survives on the subject, yet we can plainly see in his residence that he wished to create for himself an English image of country house aristocracy. This was not odd at all but a completely English ideal. Here, the concept was carried out expansively. Drayton Hall probably began to take shape in the late 1730s or early 1740s; no one knows exactly when. Governor John Drayton, a grandson, wrote that Drayton built the house at a young age, but, as a rule, projects of this kind often took ten years or twenty or more, and even then the original scheme was sometimes modified or never really finished. The earliest written record of the house is dated 1758, when it was called "Mr. Drayton's Palace," but John Drayton was living there some years before that, in the fall of 1742.

It was a house for a man who wished to single himself out, and it remains a striking sight even today, stripped of most of its original surroundings and carefully preserved in a state resembling abandonment. Architectural historians usually agree that the style is Anglo-Palladian, an "English" house designed according to the neoclassical principles of the Italian Andrea Palladio. It seems to have an American flavor to it, although the tendency to label it Caribbean finds no support whatsoever in buildings known to have been erected in eighteenth-century Barbados or Jamaica. Drayton Hall is also called Georgian, but the strongest analogy is to buildings in England constructed during the reign of Charles I, in the century before; thus, it is Carolinian Palladian and not Georgian Palladian, but Anglo-Palladian all the same. Such a connection to the time of Charles I is supported by surviving decorative detailing inside the house based in part on plates published in 1727 by William Kent in his *Designs of Inigo Jones*. Besides showing the direct borrowing of ideas from Kent's own particular rendition of Inigo Jones's style, Drayton Hall seems even more Jones-like when compared with the architect's own sketches for Whitehall in London and those by his pupil John Webb. William H. Toms's view of Charleston, published in 1739, shows what were once many buildings with an architectural character similar to Drayton Hall.

For what it was and where it was, it was a magnificent house. Drayton's architectural message is still loud and clear. The broad site lies almost level with the river, and the house stands abrupt and proud. An old, undated drawing shows a more extensive house than survives at Drayton Hall. The building we know today is shown flanked by great matching wings like those on English houses of the time, and each is surmounted by a cupola and tied to the main block by low colonnades. Other mansions on the Ashley had similar wings, but the wings actually built on Drayton Hall were ordinary plantation outbuildings of brick. Perhaps John Drayton got tired of building and gave up, or his building project outlived him. Archaeological digging has yielded evidence of connecting walls but not colonnades. In the basement a large stack of stone architectural parts has gathered dust for many years. Perhaps they were for the wings, perhaps for an elaborate gate, never built.

The facade on the riverfront is rich in the redness of its fine, delicate brickwork, which is punctuated with wooden window hoods, pilasters, and window frames. Two stories of living space and a deep attic are mounted on a high English basement containing kitchens and the like. A pair of stone stairs rise in leisurely progression to a simple pedimented doorway. On the landing one can turn and see the Ashley and the shallow-terraced ground that once was a garden. On the opposite side, away from the river, the land front presents more stone stairs that lead to deep double-stacked porches with rows of stone columns. The lower of these lofty, airy porches presents

This pile of carved stone architectural parts has long rested in the basement of Drayton Hall, in the great central room—unused elements in some forgotten grand scheme (Gordon Beall)

an uncovered apron floored in a checkerboard of stone, rather like a protruding tribunal, where the family could ceremonially receive its callers.

Documentation of Drayton Hall is frail. That Drayton and his family were living there in 1742 comes only from the tradition that the son William Henry, called Billy, was born there, and he was born in that year. Very little is known about the estate during the eighteenth century, although the physical remains suggest grandeur—the monumental house, the ruined orangery, the scaling paint on paneling in the rooms, the grand stairs in the stately entrance hall, the shell of the elegant privy—and pose the question of what the full picture must have been. A story has long persisted among the Draytons that at some point in the nineteenth century seven trunks of papers from the attic were dumped into the Ashley River. This is the only available explanation for what must have happened to the letters and other written materials that described many details of life during the first generation at Drayton Hall.

We know some things. Drayton acquired silver of great value and in large quantity. His rooms contained carved mahogany furniture. A table that survives is an elegant marble-topped rectangular piece of the Chippendale type, perhaps a serving table. The skeleton of its mate is still in the house. Drayton's beds were richly furnished with curtains and linens. Thomas Elfe, the best of the eighteenth-century Charleston cabinetmak-

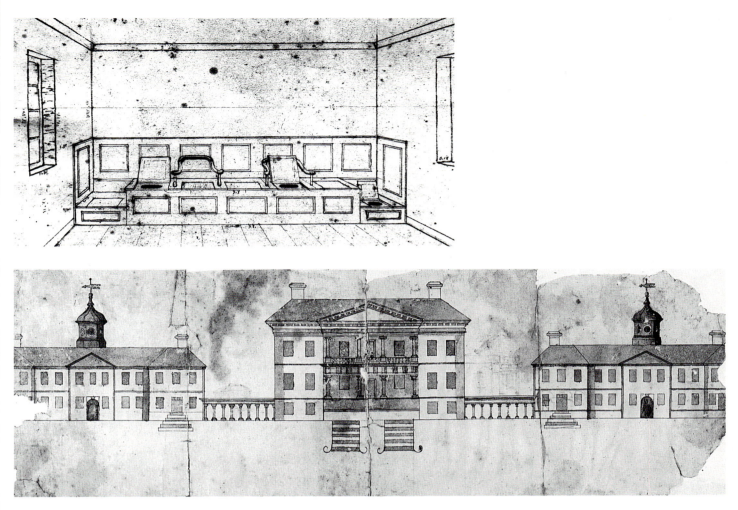

ers, often repaired furniture for Drayton and listed in his account book such items as tea tables. Once he went to mend and hang tapestries. If these hangings were actual woven tapestries, as the invoice implies, and not merely fabric wall hangings, they may have been unique in American colonial houses. Situated between the house and the river, the garden had some twelve acres. Sea captains are said to have brought exotic plants to Drayton. Live oaks, wild cherry, cedar, cypress, pine, and other native trees set aside when the site was cleared provided a parklike setting and shade.

John Drayton was married four times. His first wife, Sarah Cattell, died when he was only twenty-four, leaving him with two boys who soon followed their mother. Drayton Hall may have been started between this marriage and the next. The second wife, Charlotta Bull, four years his junior, gave birth to two more sons, William Henry and Charles, and died when Drayton was twenty-eight; she is believed to have lived in the new house. Drayton married his third wife, Margaret Glen, nine years later. She brought to the marriage her own considerable wealth and lived twenty years, producing two more boys. Her successor, and the last wife, was Rebecca Perry, she sixteen, he sixty. They had three children, two of them girls, in a brief marriage of four years that ended with Drayton's death in 1779 at the age of sixty-four. The widow lived to be eighty-one but not at Drayton Hall.

John Drayton's life paralleled years of growth and prosperity for

Top: An 1850s sketch shows the eighteenth-century privy at Drayton Hall before it was changed after the Civil War. Neatly white-washed, the room features finely designed and crafted seats, complete with arm rests. A brick-lined trough underneath admitted cleansing water and lye. Above: No specific documentation exists for this early drawing of the house's land side, but it envisions a far grander ensemble than was built. Whether this five-part scheme was John Drayton's original intention is not known (both, Historic Charleston Foundation)

Charleston and the Low Country. A review of the newspapers of the decades from the 1740s to the 1760s gives a taste of a region becoming satisfied with itself, and it has remained so for a long time. Drayton knew from his forebears' experiences the importance of political strength. The Goose Creek Party supplied a base of power, making him, at twenty-three, an officer in his parish. He was thirty-eight when appointed both an assistant judge of the court of general sessions and a justice of the court of common pleas. His position in the colony was crowned when he was thirty-nine by membership on the governor's council, the highest recognition a citizen of the colonies could receive. His public work took him to Charleston frequently, and like most rich planters he had several boats, probably including the typical barge with an awning, a vessel his male slaves rowed or poled downriver to town, easing their master's trip.

High public position in the eighteenth century required that a man live in some state, himself appropriately wigged and groomed, and his lady in silk, when the occasion required it. No descriptions have come down to us of Drayton's mode of hospitality, but one can read colonial splendor in his house today even in empty rooms. It accommodated many guests. The dining room is long, with a handsomely finished wood-paneled interior and a broad fireplace at one end that could receive saw logs on a cold night. Plantation cooks mingled English, Caribbean, and African cuisine to make Low Country tables legendary with spicy renderings of rice, of course, and vegetables of all kinds, venison, turkey, duck, especially sea turtles from the West Indies, prepared spicy, with "Saffron and Negroe pepper." On the winding service stair that threads through the house, probably added for privacy after the house was built, servants hurried from floor to floor, bearing trays of food, clean, folded linen, and written messages, and taking and replacing bedroom pots.

At the bottom of the service stair was the basement, so called because it was above ground and the architectural base of the house externally, as opposed to being a subterranean cellar. In an eighteenth-century house this area was usually used for domestic work, including the kitchen, servants' hall, pantries, and storage rooms, and this was its purpose also at Drayton Hall. The basement's great central room is somewhat more than the servants' hall one might expect to find in that location. It is large for a servants' gathering place, and it seems too intrusively situated for a banquet kitchen. Something about it, the stone floor, the mighty fireplace, is more gala than utilitarian. The plan of the basement makes special deference to this room, suggesting that it was not intended for servitors but for people who were themselves served. In adjacent corridors, for example, are built-in buffets, like niches, English features characteristic not of basements but of halls outside dining rooms on the principal floors. Perhaps it was a breezy family dining room for summer and in the autumn a supper room to serve the festive hunting parties in which the colonial South Carolinians took delight. It must have been designed with this use in mind. But houses, of course, are not always lived in as they were intended to be, and

Opposite: The entrance hall, with its magnificent double staircase of mahogany and pine, is on the river front and leads to the principal rooms upstairs. In the eighteenth century most visitors came to Drayton Hall by boat, alighting at the landing on the Ashley River and then walking through gardens to the house (Gordon Beall)

the basement in fact may never have been used for anything but work space.

John Drayton, a busy man of affairs, presided over a family that seems often to have been unhappy. It was never more so than when the eldest son, William Henry, returned from school in England. As the eldest son he was the one who was to inherit the fortune, and to an Englishman law study was considered the best preparation for estate management. Expected to learn to be a planter, William Henry instead was bookish by inclination. He had taken to the law in a big way. Back home he announced his intention to set up a practice. Old Drayton was not pleased. William Henry was strong, like his father, and the two clashed. Seeds of bitter memories were sown. Many years after both were dead, William Henry Drayton's son remembered that the grandfather "was a man of indifferent education, of a confined mind, proud and stingy. . . . [S]uch was his character that he lived in riches, but without public esteem." So bitter a judgment by one who had been a little boy in the household went unchallenged by other family members who also knew the patriarch as dark and stormy. "I cannot bear slights from my children," John Drayton wrote in 1771, when William Henry was twenty-nine. Tensions in the home circle cannot have been relaxed by the introduction of the sixteen-year-old stepmother four years later. John Drayton's sons described her to their own sons, inaccurately, as low born.

William Henry Drayton remained in his father's house, a perpetual child in John Drayton's eyes. The father was determined to rule, and the son, it seemed, could never please him. To an outsider's view William Henry, although devoted to his profession of law, was too much under John Drayton's thumb to go far with a career. That he selected the courtroom over agriculture must have hurt the father, who, although a judge himself, might have hoped to have in his principal heir assurance that his farming kingdom would endure. Young Drayton pursued his career anyway. He married, and two children were born to the couple. No sudden, brilliant legal achievements came to soften his father's view of him as a failure. William Henry Drayton's time had not yet come, but it would.

William Henry Drayton was the son of Drayton Hall's builder and became a leading figure in the Carolinas during the American Revolution (Drayton Hall)

On up the Atlantic coast, the Philadelphian Benjamin Chew set about building Cliveden in the 1760s, twenty years or more after Drayton Hall was occupied. It was a rich era of house building in Philadelphia and its environs; Charleston's prosperity paled beside it. By the 1760s Philadelphia was mentioned with respect throughout Britain for the astuteness of its merchants and the urbanity and well-being of its citizens. In the decade before the Revolution, Philadelphia was the second-largest city in the British empire, a sprawling urban grid of prim brick and wood houses, green squares, and several tall steeples—not the least the one thrusting up from the Pennsylvania State House, meeting place of the bold and outspoken assembly of the colony and a building that would be known to history as Independence Hall.

In the summer of the memorable year 1763, when the Seven Years War ended in victory for the English king over France, Elizabeth and Benjamin Chew and their children spent several idyllic months at the country home of their friend Judge William Allen, six miles from Philadelphia, near Germantown. Judge Allen, probably the freest spender of Philadelphia's conspicuous upper class, was in England on a visit. He gave his younger friends the key to his beautiful mansion, Mount Airy. So happy were the Chews with their escape that they soon imagined themselves owning a country house in this healthful and pretty spot. They looked for land to buy. In July of that year Chew paid £650 for eleven acres just down the road from Judge Allen. The promising site sloped up from the Germantown road, providing a pedestal along a fine ridge that Benjamin Chew meant to adorn with a dream house to which he could escape from the rigors of life in Philadelphia. In the fall the Chews were back home in their house on South Front Street, several blocks from the Philadelphia wharves, when Judge Allen wrote to them, "It gives me pleasure . . . that you are like to build and be my neighbor."

Owning a country house was fashionable among the Philadelphia gentry. In the late 1760s one could walk comfortably from the waterfront to open country, leaving the grid of the city and its 22,000 inhabitants behind. Such wealthy men as William Allen and his friends the McPhersons, the Norrises, the Dickinsons, the Mifflins, the Shippens, and the Hamiltons, among others, lived between town houses and suburban estates, where their houses—some pretentious, some not at all—were surrounded by gardens and orchards. This custom was really a mark of the urbanization of the city, for the previous generation had stayed close to town. It was also a reflection of fashionable London, where for fifty years and more rich merchants and professionals had built part-time residences in villages along the Thames, about the same distance from London as Germantown was from Philadelphia. Some of these houses were free-standing, squarish structures of two or three stories, perhaps five bays wide, steep roofed, with a decorated doorway in the center. They still can be seen along old streets in Hampstead, Peckham, Chamberwell, Greenwich, Clapton, and other villages an easy river trip from London, and in many ways they recall the characteristic boxlike American colonial mansion. To Londoners these houses were holiday retreats; but the Philadelphians' estates also were farms, and in their bounty the city folk took special interest and pride.

Benjamin Chew, attorney general of the Pennsylvania colony, a Marylander by birth, had come from wealth and made more. At age forty-one in 1763 he was counted among the high gentry—if that word really applied at all to Americans—and well before middle age he achieved prominence in private practice and public service. He read law under his father, once the chief justice of what is now Delaware, known then as the "lower counties" of Pennsylvania. Moved to Philadelphia, his father put him in the office of the irascible Andrew Hamilton, a famous lawyer there and the power behind the construction of the Pennsylvania State House. Chew

Top: Benjamin Chew approved every detail of his house, ordering the decorative roof urns from an English catalogue of stone ornaments (Jack E. Boucher, Historic American Buildings Survey). Above: Chief Justice Chew is seen here in a silhouette on a desk at Cliveden (Erik Kvalsvik). Right: Elizabeth Oswald Chew, Benjamin's second wife, enjoyed Cliveden as a country retreat that suited their large family (Chester County Historical Society)

spent one year at Middle Temple in London at twenty-one. No young American could have been better trained for a bright future. And he was a lucky man.

Back home he gained attention in public affairs as a strong traditionalist and was soon noticed by the mighty Penn family of proprietors. They made him their lawyer, the legal protector of their vast holdings in American real estate. Chew turned from the Quaker meeting of his youth to the Church of England, to join on the Sabbath the new men of power and influence in Philadelphia. He was present at the prophetic Albany Congress in 1754, where the delegates from parts of New England and the Middle Atlantic colonies proposed the formation of a central government in

North America. With the interest of his Philadelphia clients well in mind, he took an active role in land settlements with the Indian tribes. His appointment as attorney general made him the chief law officer of the colony. No others among the famous Philadelphia lawyers had made so meteoric an ascent.

Elizabeth Chew was his second wife, a woman still in her twenties in 1763. Her portrait captures both good looks and a sense of humor, an oval face and expressive eyes, a long neck and delicate, tapering hands. Chew's first wife died young, leaving him a widower of thirty-three with four little girls. He courted and won Elizabeth Oswald two years later, hardly time enough to put away mourning bands and locks of the hair of the departed. Yet he had a family to raise. Elizabeth and Benjamin Chew had a son and seven daughters. A second son, the infant Joseph, died soon after the summer at Judge Allen's. The household eventually boasted twelve children all living under the happiest circumstances.

Chew's friends agreed that it was time for him to build a country house, not only to escape the city heat and diseases, but also to express his position in a way any Englishman might. Occupied though he was with work, Chew fell comfortably into that most gentlemanly pastime of house planning. John Drayton left us almost nothing on paper about Drayton Hall, but attorney Chew left an abundance. A file of drawings shows us several different ideas he developed. For advice he called in his friend William Peters, whose magnificent house on the Schuylkill River was one of the ornaments of the colony. As any of us is likely to do today when we intend to build, Chew clipped pictures he liked from magazines. William Kent's Kew House in Surry, built 1731–1735 for the Prince of Wales, appeared in the popular *Gentleman's Magazine and Historical Chronicles,* published during Chew's summer at Judge Allen's. The clipping is preserved in Chew's bundle of plans. Chew spread out these same papers for his children to see, and they one day told their children that Cliveden was an exact copy of the prince's palace at Kew.

Chew experimented with several schemes, all predictably Anglo-Palladian. None of his plans rivaled that of John Drayton in grandeur or in the profusion of rooms that would require many servants in attendance. He wanted a fine but very forthright house. Chew consulted English architectural pattern books of the time, perhaps James Gibbs's influential *A Book of Architecture* (London, 1728). Liking Kent's work, perhaps he also studied the Inigo Jones volume that Drayton had used. When his ideas took shape, he gave his drawings to a professional builder. In October 1763 Chew made an agreement with John Hesser, a stonemason who was one of the Germans of Germantown. Hesser received a £25 deposit to accomplish as much as he could through the fall and winter, in preparation for the spring thaw, when building could begin. April 1764 saw the ground broken and the cellar dug. Chew made his payments regularly, recording each in a leatherbound book that he had set aside for the purpose—today gathered with his plans and letters in the Chew family papers at the Historical Society of Pennsylvania.

Cliveden's stone walls rose fast. In November Hesser called for the first measurement. This was an ancient procedure for payment in construction work that was still universal in the eighteenth century, before craftsmen became hourly wage earners in the nineteenth. The measurer, agreed on in advance by client and tradesman, was summoned when both parties were satisfied with the quality of the work that had been done. This individual applied a special formula, usually measuring cubic volume to determine the amount of payment due. The process made more sense than it might seem, for the estimates of cost and the bids were figured on the same cubic basis; thus, the two were likely to be close. Nor was the level of quality a thing to be negotiated after the job was done—the endless frustration today in added costs for repeat work. The measurer, because he had been appointed early on, had considerable financial credibility in the work, and his judgment usually held up in court. At Cliveden the principal measurer was Jacob Knor, Chew's carpenter and a man involved in many aspects of the building, assisted by Jacob Lewis, probably his lumber supplier.

Benjamin Chew paid the high price of £357 17s. 9d. for the completed stonework on the front of his house, which was dressed stone in uniform rectangular blocks called ashlar. Some of the other walls, described as "common," were less costly rubble, composed of odd-sized stones; this base was smoothed over with a coat of stucco, which was scored to match the ashlar on the front. Jacob Lewis called for measurement on the windows by winter, and the roof of heavy timber frame and wood shingles was in place that fall of 1764. With the house closed in, most of the work could proceed year-round.

For two years more the builders labored on Cliveden, and the house was completed by Christmas 1767. Workmen made interior window shutters, laid flooring, installed carved woodwork, and painted the rooms. Big fires dried the plaster, as was the common custom when work extended into the cool season or when summer shed an inordinate amount of rain. Chew's fuel cost was high, so the large fireplaces must have brimmed. Another cost was the party for his workmen when the house was closed in. This he paid for, providing food and drink on the site.

Although weighted down with work in Philadelphia, Chew must have anticipated with special joy his trips to the construction site. It was about a two-hour carriage ride, if the weather was fair. To build a house is a major passage in anyone's life, and it happens to few people today. He took great pride in his house. The tone of the place was important to him. Being a good Philadelphian, he responded to simplicity of the substantial sort, and simplicity befitted his position as a jurist and serious leader in the colony. But even he yielded to a little ornament. In the month the construction crew left, Chew ordered carved stone urns from England, ornamental elements rather like finials to decorate his roof—a concept he had no doubt seen somewhere, for he incorporated the idea into his drawings at the start. "I have shown the pattern of the urns," he wrote to his English supplier, ". . . to the knowing ones among us and have fixed on [catalogue

Above: The parlor at Cliveden has fine Georgian wood detailing and a fireplace facing of Pennsylvania blue "King of Prussia" marble. Furnishings are placed as they were when the last Chew lived here, two hundred years after the first. Left: Over the sheen of old pine floors, the stair hall leads through the column screen into the entrance hall. Opposite: Cliveden's small reception parlor is seen through a pedimented doorway from the entrance hall. The handsome desk of mahogany dates to the time of Benjamin and Elizabeth Chew, while the neoclassical chairs probably were acquired by a later generation; one of the chairs appears in the nineteenth-century view of Cliveden on page 35 (all, Erik Kvalsvik)

design] No. 2, only that it is to have little or no carve work as most suitable to the plainness of my building." The house was improved in smaller ways nearly constantly for another decade.

Chew's interest in Cliveden was shared by Elizabeth Chew, and they both had much of which to be proud. Cliveden presented a bold, crisp face to Germantown Avenue. The stone is really the art of this house. The uniform ashlar blocks are native Wissahickon stone, an iridescent schist layered with visible strata. A vaguely purple cast enriches the gray-brown color according to the nuances of light, and the effect is forced to some extent by the current white paint of the fine wood trim. Inside, Cliveden has come down to us in general probably much as it was in the eighteenth century, although one suspects the presence of some Victorian alterations in the colonial style, perhaps made in the middle to third quarter of the nineteenth century. One enters into a broad saloon—more than an entrance hall—with an easy flight of stairs seen in a hall beyond it through a screen of wooden columns. The plan unfolds from this central T-shaped configuration of reception and stair spaces. The parlor and dining room are to the rear as in the Annapolis houses with which Chew was probably familiar. Cliveden is a house of high ceilings and effective cross-ventilation that must have made it comfortable in the summer. Yet it is a formal house, with an ample parlor.

As with Drayton Hall, it is easy to spend hours studying Cliveden and speculating on the life there. Unlike Drayton Hall, it was originally a part-time house that was not always surrounded by people and was unused for part of the year and thus vulnerable to robberies. The plan indicates that it was guarded whether or not the Chews were there. To the left of the entrance hall is a small room without a fireplace, in all likelihood the eighteenth-century porter's lodge—an inside "safe" and gatehouse—occupied by an employee or slave who lived there year-round. These porter's or doorkeeper's chambers were common in England, and several other American examples are found in Maryland; the one built at the White House forty years later is still in use. In rooms like these, valuables were stored: books and papers, silver, jewelry, and the like. The steward or porter who slept there kept a loaded pistol for protection. In case of fire he could easily take the silver and documents outside to safety. At Cliveden, when there was no resident porter, the shutters of its safe room were always kept closed and valuable things were stored there, notably in recent times some of the voluminous and precious Chew family papers.

Benjamin Chew acquired all of the ornaments of wealth—town house, country house, handsome coach—and was usually hard up for cash. Bills often stayed on hand quite a while before they were paid. Even so, he received cash salaries for his jobs in public service and also claimed quite large legal fees from private clients. The Chew farms and plantations in Delaware and Maryland must have occasionally turned profits, as they would in later years, notwithstanding the perils of absentee ownership. Chew was a professional man whose membership in the colonial landed gentry was secondary. Although he was a planter and slaveholder down

Like other good and loyal subjects of the king, Benjamin and Elizabeth Chew enjoyed their English tea. Here their chairs are pulled up to their tea table in a corner of Cliveden's parlor, set with dishes acquired by their son (Erik Kvalsvik)

south, and his heirs also would be until the Civil War, his main income seems to have derived from his law clients, notably the Penn family. The Penns' American business endeavors he managed entirely, from rental properties, to frequent lawsuits over the estate's many legal claims against the infringements of others, to the quiet transfer by the 1770s of some of its colonial capital home to England.

This was an adoring family circle. Elizabeth Chew willingly took the domestic role and seems to have lived happily in the circumstances of life Chew provided. She was a good and devoted mother to Chew's four daughters by his first wife. She liked to take the family to Cliveden, of which she became genuinely fond. "[I]f you had but have been with us," she wrote to her husband in 1768, "I would have enjoyed Cliffden with much higher satisfaction than ever for I really think the absence of a few days gives it new beauties." Now and then she worried about expenses and how the stream of bills ran so much faster than the incoming cash. She wrote that she "must check her growing attachments" for Cliveden, "for now and then a melancholy thought of who will succeed me & its being let out for a lake house as you sometimes say it must be, forbid me wishing to make those little improvements I think I could."

They did live well. Chew had liked fine things since his youth. He acquired furniture through the years, patronizing Philadelphia cabinetmakers and those in Germantown. The elegant pieces were hauled out in late spring from the house in town, then returned in the fall. Once the transfer included embellishments such as looking glasses and beds. Chew's purchase in 1771 of Governor Penn's mansion in town provided some furniture later used at Cliveden, including magnificent American appointments assembled during the Penn tenure. Penn's house, with its furnishings and large garden, was considered one of the grandest in the city; it was built by William Byrd III, the rich gambling heir of the famous eighteenth-century planter-diarist whose Virginia mansion, Westover, overlooks the James River.

In 1774 Benjamin Chew succeeded to the august post formerly occupied by his friend and mentor, Judge Allen, becoming the crown's supreme legal official in the colony. The city had doubled in size since Chew had started Cliveden. It was often pointed out by Europeans as a place where democracy worked. Dublin, for example, liked to refer to itself as "Philadelphian" in the 1770s. By that time, Quaker simplicity, still the rule in Philadelphia, was in high circles sometimes flavored with Anglican opulence. The Chews lived between their two houses in an elegant state after 1774, as befit the chief justice of Pennsylvania. Vincent Ducomb, hairdresser, was paid an annual salary to exercise his art on the principal Chew heads; powder, pomades, and ribbons were listed among his supplies. Elegant fabrics and millinery decorations are recorded in the account books, along with costly food and wines. The Chews had a domestic staff of about ten slaves and some free whites, including a coachman, a cook, and a gardener. Slaves, it would appear, performed only the personal services, one being Chew's "body servant." An elaborately dressed "English servant," probably under an indenture for services, ran away from the Chews in 1775, and Chew advertised for his capture.

Thirty or forty years before citizens of the Atlantic coast such as Drayton and Chew began to develop their aristocracies and borrowed emblems of civilization, Ambrose Madison, with the appetite of the age for acquiring land, ventured into the hard wilderness, into the back country of Virginia. Although he was considered a gentleman, he does not compare comfortably with Drayton or Chew, nor does he contrast in any useful way. Not so much in the English mold, Madison was more a pioneer, as the character of this breed would be understood more clearly later on, given to daring and experiment. The ability to dream he shared with the other two. Madison was a planter and slave owner who wanted to better his economic state. In 1723 he and his brother-in-law Thomas Chew, probably a distant Maryland cousin of Benjamin Chew, gained title by patent to 4,675 acres in Orange County, Virginia. This heavily wooded country, sparsely settled, still threatened newcomers with dangers from Indian attacks. But it beckoned with agricultural promise. It presented almost the antithesis of the familiar, level Tidewater region (as Virginia's low country was called), for the terrain rolled into foothills and at last into the Blue Ridge Mountains, a curtain across deeper mystery beyond.

Ambrose Madison had set himself to farming and built a dwelling on his land by the time of his death in 1732. The end must have come suddenly, for his business house was not in order. He and Chew had never made a division of it, and by the original agreement the entire tract became, on Madison's death, Chew's property. The issue went unsettled for five years. Chew was at last generous. He divided the property in half, giving one part to the widow, Frances, and her nine-year-old son, James. The boy grew up to love land even more than had his father. He married Nelly Conway, a strong-willed Tidewater woman, and busied himself untiringly with business. Virginia county courthouses of Orange, Louisa, and Culpeper record his acquisitions of land parcels large and small, his purchases, his swaps, his presence at sheriffs' auctions. He built on his father's holdings in slaves and tilled the land his father had settled.

He also occupied his father's house, about which we know nothing, except to suspect that it was simple shelter. When Nelly Madison was expecting their first child in 1751, she journeyed fifty miles home to her mother. Here at remote Conway's Crossing, near the ferry that crossed the Rappahannock River to the town of Port Royal, Virginia, she gave birth to a son, James Madison, Jr.—the father of the Constitution of the as-yet-unimagined United States and the fourth president of the nation it created. Eleven other children followed over the next twenty-three years, seven of whom lived to maturity. In 1755 the Madisons began construction of a new house built of brick. It was a good house, set two stories high over a basement, each floor having a center hall and two rooms on each side. From its doorway the land spread to the feet of the Blue Ridge, giving a dreamlike, unforgettable view. This building still exists in part, buried in the walls of a much-expanded house. Most of the children appear to have been born here, in comfortable plastered and wainscoted rooms.

During the years in which young James grew up, James and Nelly Madison prospered. At some point they began to call their farm Montpelier. They looked after each other devotedly, an affection they continued for the rest of their long lives. The small and wiry Madison must have seen himself in his eldest son. The boy was precocious, already copying poems in a notebook at the age of eight and reading the older Madison's issues of *The Spectator*. His father seems to have realized that the lad had something special, some gifts that elevated him above the plow and the land deed. He sent James away to a Scots schoolmaster when he was about twelve, and as a boarder the boy studied Latin, developing quickly into a teenager who spent his money buying the works of Virgil, Horace, Cicero, and Justinian. Of all of the teachers—many of them famous men—who would instruct James Madison, he would one day place the greatest value on his years with Donald Robertson.

After studying for some time at home under a tutor, young Madison entered what is now Princeton at the age of nineteen. Here, under what were considered the best teaching minds in the colonies, he briefly courted the idea of an ecclesiastical career before becoming immersed in the philosophical and legal writing of the Enlightenment. Politics was the talk of the hour at college, and while a frail, sickly Madison avoided the roughhouse aspects of school, in the discussions he gained the respect of his fellow students and took particular interest in the subject of religious reform. From the Presbyterian environment of Princeton, he looked toward home with dismay on the Church of England in Virginia, which he determined was a crumbling edifice. He returned home with his eyes opened.

Reading law at Montpelier, Madison did take an interest in farming, although his pragmatic parents kept a firm hand on the busy activities of the working farm that surrounded him. And while it would appear that Madison's Orange County was on the other side of the moon, he found himself in the midst of the coming political crisis. The tensions of the times were felt in Orange, almost as soon as in the cities on the coast. To a college friend living in Philadelphia James Madison wrote from Montpelier in the summer of 1774: "As to the sentiments of the people of this Colony with respect to the Bostonians I can assure I find them generally very warm in their favor. The Natives are very unanimous and resolute, are making resolves in almost every County and I believe are willing to fall in with the Other Colonies in any expedient measure."

James Madison was painted in silhouette by Joseph Sansom (Perot Collection, Historical Society of Pennsylvania)

The work of a chain of colonial committees of correspondence led to the meeting of the Continental Congress in Philadelphia in the fall. In December the Boston Tea Party became a violent climax to the New England boycotts against British goods. The winds of change had risen to blow full force through the minds of Americans. There were fence sitters, but few Americans could simply turn away. And what was the course taken by those who lived at Drayton Hall, Cliveden, and Montpelier?

Down south in Carolina, William Henry Drayton, incensed by Britain's actions, emerged from Drayton Hall and joined the local committee of correspondence in Charleston, quickly becoming its president. He was suddenly the center of things, his pen flying in the creation of patriotic essays, his time filled with politicking that took him even into the remote Upcountry. In a sense, William Henry never returned home after that. Possessed now with a high purpose, he quickly rose to public stature far greater than anyone had ever dreamed. John Drayton's views of this change are not recorded.

James Madison, not yet twenty-five, joined his father on Orange County's committee of public safety. He was made a colonel, his only distinction of that sort until that unimaginable time far distant, in 1812, when he would be commander-in-chief as the British returned to America. Young Madison was on fire with the events of the day. He wrote of his home county: "We are very busy at present in raising men and procuring the necessaries for defending ourselves and our fr[i]ends in case of a sudden invasion. . . . There will by Spring, I expect, be some thousands of well-trained men High Spirited men ready to meet danger, whenever it appears, who are influenced by no mercenary Principles, bearing their own expenses and having the prospect of no recompence but the honour and safety of their Country."

Benjamin Chew, an older and, in theory, a wiser man, hesitated. Walking brick sidewalks to and from his town house, a few blocks from the State House where the Continental Congress sat, he considered and reconsidered the events that were flashing before him. To defy lawful authority was against all he stood for. He looked for a way out for Pennsylvania. As the premier symbol of British legal authority then in a hostile Philadelphia, he must have cherished the peace of escape to Cliveden, removed from turmoil. In town, members of the Continental Congress passed through his doors as guests. He was on familiar ground with some of the most articulate of the revolutionary thinkers, but then he had always been shrewd about his position. Chew marveled to observe that although war drums were beating, in the law the colonial citizens were acting with cool reason. He knew his own loyalties were the subject of whispering among all classes in the city, and he realized that in time he would have to commit himself one way or another. The decision came slowly. At last he took his stand in April 1776, three months before the Declaration of Independence, and issued from his bench a dramatic interpretation of the law wholly unexpected to all who heard it—one that was to give legal status to the Americans' next actions.

A spectator recorded the emotional scene. Judge Chew, in the course of charging a grand jury in a case involving treason, was explaining from the bench the character of treason by law, when one of the jurymen stepped boldly forward, interrupted him, and asked, in the context of a turbulent Philadelphia, "What then is to become of us who are now opposing the arbitrary power attempted to be exercised by the British Ministry?"

Chew paused only a moment and replied: "I have stated that an opposition of force of arms to the lawful authority of the King or his Ministers is High Treason; but the moment when the King or his ministers shall exceed the constitutional authority vested in them by the constitution, submission to their mandates becomes Treason." This most loyal of Englishmen now justified a revolution against not England, but those who ruled it.

Benjamin Chew's silhouette is the earliest image of the chief justice at Cliveden (Cliveden, Inc.)

Children of the Revolution

George Washington was inaugurated as president of the United States on April 14, 1789, at Federal Hall in New York City. Three months later the fall of the Bastille in Paris signaled the revolutionary age in Europe. This event changed more but accomplished less than the colonists' relatively gentle upheaval. Americans might claim that the Revolution had not altered their lives. But it had. Men-at-arms had moved across the map as though there were no colonial borders. Citizens looked inland toward and over the mountains instead of out to sea. War and the spirit of the moment had bound the thirteen islands more closely.

If William Henry Drayton had lived only a few years more, his political abilities in South Carolina might have qualified him for the more august forums in Philadelphia. He might justifiably have had his place reserved among the dignitaries at Federal Hall watching Washington at that first inaugural. As it happened, William Henry and John Drayton died three years after independence, the son first, but within a few months of each other. Five years later, in 1784, the quiet brother, Charles, now the heir, dispatched forever his father's young widow, by then twenty years old, through an enticing trade of furniture and plate from Drayton Hall and established himself in John Drayton's shoes. He was a physician by training, a milder man than his father or brother, and his diary chronicles a blissful life as a successful planter who kept his mansion in good repair—but, alas, did not much else. His heirs would own it for 190 years more.

Benjamin Chew was not at Federal Hall, although alive and thriving in 1789. Accused of Tory sympathies and incarcerated comfortably for some time, he had, as always, landed firmly on his feet once the shouting was over. This time it was a wonder, however. His pretty teenage daughters had danced with the British invaders and flirted with the same poetic Major André whom Washington hanged as a spy.

Even Chew's lovely Cliveden had, with its thick stone walls, shown favor to the enemy. On October 4, 1777, in the early morning fog, the mansion stood as a British fortress ruining General Washington's siege of Germantown, a phase of his promising plan to drive the invaders from

Not long after British troops successfully defended Cliveden against George Washington's soldiers, an unknown British artist recorded the events of the day in The Storming of the Chew House *(Cliveden, Inc.)*

Philadelphia. Three companies of the British Fortieth Regiment of Foot were ordered to take cover in Cliveden, and Washington gave the order to remove the "annoyance" before he would permit his Continentals and militia to march on. The three hours or so of unexpected fighting at Chew's house, in which the British held their own, confused things sufficiently to guarantee an American disaster in the Battle of Germantown, during which nearly a thousand died on both sides. Benjamin Chew, Jr., went to Cliveden after the battle and reported to his father a scene of utter devastation.

The extent of the damage is unclear today. Scars from cannonballs can still be seen on the walls of the entrance hall. The original front doors, smashed by musket and bayonet, were lost only when the carriage house in which they were stored burned in 1970. Cliveden is a solid house, but it is not known exactly how much Chew was inclined to repair its battle scars two hundred years ago. He sold it to a merchant named Blair McClenachan. This young and successful Irishman, a privateer, made Cliveden his home for eighteen years. Then he sold it back to Benjamin Chew, apparently in a better state of restoration, and Chew's family lived on there until 1972.

While that diminutive powerhouse, father Madison, plowed, sowed, and harvested his fields throughout the Revolution and the brief ensuing period of the Confederation, his eldest son, James, drew closer to the centers of power. James Madison was a hard, constant worker, like his father, but in quite another way. His sharp mind recommended him to ever more important national participation. A delegate from Virginia to the Constitutional Convention in Philadelphia, he became the principal architect of the new instrument of government. His deep learning in ancient and modern history made up for his unimpressive presence and his shortcomings as a public speaker. He labored on the new Constitution, putting forth those ideas of the Enlightenment that he and Jefferson and their circle found so perfectly suited to American life. The framers of the Constitution had determined to let history be their guide in organizing a new national government, and they found Madison's intellect and common sense compelling. At crossroads, when practicality and personal interest challenged loftier goals, Madison drew the compromises. So significant was his part that he was considered the guiding force behind the written document that still binds the states of the Union. If anyone standing by in Wall Street watching the first president take his oath felt that his heart and soul were more of that moment than perhaps any other person's, it must have been James Madison.

He is remembered as being a somewhat peculiar man, a small, thin figure like his father, only dressed always in black, seemingly lost in his philosophies. Contemporaries sometimes implied that he was priggish and withdrawn from society. Yet Madison's friendships were warm and numerous.

In any but the most casual company he was likely to become the center of conversation, more really than Jefferson or Monroe or Hamilton or the elder Adams. People listened, knowing that he had wise and often witty things to say. At forty-three he was, although a frail fellow to see, one of the giants of Congress in the dawning days of the Republic.

A single man, he courted women with some ardor when the federal government was in New York, then Philadelphia. And no woman did he pursue with more vigor than the Quaker woman he married, Dolley Payne Todd. The pert widow seemed the utter opposite of him. In the spring of 1794, when they met, she was twenty-five, alone no more than a half year, living with her young son, Payne Todd, in a brick house at the corner of Walnut and Fourth streets in Philadelphia. Like many other men, Madison had admired her from afar. Her domestic environment, although wholly Quaker, was not without notoriety in the capital, for she—only a few months in weeds—was already receiving men callers, and her fifteen-year-old sister, Lucy, had eloped with Steptoe Washington, the president's rakish nephew. Far from repelled, James Madison wanted a closer look. "Thou must come to me," an astonished widow Todd wrote to a friend, "the great little Madison has asked to be brought to see me this evening."

The attraction seems to have been instant. James and Dolley saw each other frequently through the balance of the spring, and by summer, when Dolley went to Virginia to take the healthful waters, one of Madison's intimates wrote to her that he "thinks so much of you in the day that he has Lost his Tongue, at Night he Dreams of you & Starts in his Sleep a Calling on you to relieve his Flame for he Burns to such an excess that he will be shortly consumed." Five months after they met, they were quietly married, with no prior announcement, at Steptoe and Lucy Washington's farm in Virginia. On her wedding day, September 15, 1794, Dolley wrote: "[T]his day I give my Hand to the Man who of all other's I most admire. In this Union I have every thing that is soothing and greatful in prospect—& my little Payne will have a generous & tender protector." She had trod the paths of love and marriage before, and her eyes were wide open. The bridegroom was in love to abandon. Wrote the bride to a girlfriend the day after her marriage: "Dolley Madison! Alass."

Within the week they journeyed to Middletown, Virginia, to visit his sister, Nelly Hite, who, with her husband, Isaac, was prospering on a 554-acre farm in the Shenandoah Valley. That late September their farm must have been resplendent, with its high fields of wheat and orchards of apples. Madison's brother-in-law worked his farm with slaves and hired hands and was a shrewd farmer. His grandfather, like Ambrose Madison, had come to his region early and had acquired extensive lands, including this farm, which his grandson was to call Belle Grove (originally written Belgrove). Nelly and Isaac Hite showed the newlyweds plans they had commissioned for what Madison later described as "a large house."

James Madison was more comfortable with his books on political thought than the architectural pattern books he found on the library shelves

Above: James Madison's portrait, painted about 1792, is the work of the noted artist Charles Willson Peale (Thomas Gilcrease Institute of American History and Art/Montpelier). Opposite: This miniature of Dolley Madison by T. C. Lübbers dates from the early 1800s (New-York Historical Society)

of his friends. But he had seen enough to know something was wrong with his sister's plan. If the Hites had an architect as such it is unknown. They did have a builder, a Mr. Bond—first name thus far lost—and Madison thought he needed instruction in such matters as porticoes, one of which was proposed here. Madison offered to present the problem to Thomas Jefferson.

The Madisons returned to Philadelphia for the opening of Congress. Dolley Madison's former house, her separate property, was rented out, and Madison in turn took the first in a succession of rented houses they were to occupy during their years in the capital. With a ready-made family, James Madison now enjoyed a very different sort of life. His wife was expelled from her church for reasons not stated but probably apparent. She was not sorry, for she bore scars from her Quaker upbringing. Years later, after a tongue lashing from some Quakers, she wrote to her husband how the incident "made me recollect the times when [the Quakers] used to control me entirely and debar me from so many advantages and pleasures, and although . . . entirely from their clutches, I really felt my ancient terror of them revive."

She traded her Quaker bonnet for a stylish turban. As the woman emerged on the stage of fame, so her fondness for fashion took her farther from the meetinghouse. The Madisons' marriage soon settled into one of mutual devotion and support. They had no children together, and this fact seemed to draw them closer. She supplemented him in his extremes and he in hers. In the near-perfect melding there was no room for Dolley's son, Payne Todd. As an adult he took bitter revenge on his mother for putting him in second place.

True to his word, Madison laid the house-building difficulties of Nelly and Isaac Hite before Jefferson, who was then secretary of state and probably Madison's closest friend. Jefferson's affection for building was well known at that time, mainly for the peculiar Roman temple form of the Virginia capitol then rising in Richmond and also, locally and to a lesser extent, for the country residences he designed for himself and his neighbors, using published design books and complicated mathematical theories of proportions. Madison's letter was presented to Jefferson in person by Mr. Bond. "On my suggestion," wrote Madison to Jefferson, Bond "is to visit Monticello not only to profit of examples before his eyes, but to ask the favor of your advice on the plan of the House. . . . In general, any hints which may occur to you for improving the place will be thankfully received."

No record exists of the meeting at Monticello. Construction of Belle Grove proceeded in the last years of the eighteenth century, with scant records kept for posterity. The long, rolling site may not have been as open as now, for the house, as its name implies, may have been in a grove of trees. Bond used some Aquia sandstone from the Potomac River for the trim but built the walls of local limestone, of the kind that formed rugged walls at places along the sides of nearby Cedar Creek. The walls might also be called German stonework, like that at Cliveden, for the trades in the valley were dominated by Germans as much as in Germantown. Similarly, the main facade of Belle Grove also is finished with orderly ashlar blocks, dressed smooth, while the other walls are irregular.

Did Jefferson design it? All that can be said for sure is that it is distinctly Jeffersonian, resembling in plan and elevation other houses he designed, most particularly Farmington in Kentucky, built at about the same time. The form was not unique to Jefferson, but he had at least an opportunity to add his touches to this house. Letters do indicate, however, that the Hites' own ideas were along the lines of what was built, before Jefferson was asked to give his views. The stylistic ambivalence of the interior, a bit Federal and a bit Georgian, shows a confusion not foreign to Jefferson's houses, but it perhaps is more comfortably attributed to a country builder with a client whose taste for the stylish and up-to-date was not wholly informed.

Belle Grove is a fine, indeed, an elegant house, always called a mansion among its farmhouse neighbors. The Hites may not have built their portico until after Nelly's death in 1802. The indomitable Isaac married again within the year. Ann Tunstall Maury Hite gave birth to ten children, making a total of twelve in the Hite family, and Belle Grove had to be expanded to shelter them. The completed house made a pretty picture on a hardworking valley farm. Even today it speaks well of the culture that built it.

Right: Two modern-day inhabitants of Belle Grove cat nap on the front portico, oblivious to the panoramic view of the Shenandoah Valley (Erik Kvalsvik). Opposite: Isaac and Nelly Hite's house of stone was designed at home, but it probably profited from some consultation by Thomas Jefferson (Ping Amranand)

Above left: Belle Grove's dining room has been refurnished with pieces typical of the region in the late eighteenth and early nineteenth centuries (Erik Kvalsvik). Above right: Nelly Madison Hite, painted with her son James, was raised at Montpelier with her brother James Madison (Belle Grove, Inc.). Left: The study at Belle Grove includes a writing chair of the Windsor type and, at the window, a heavy paneled shutter, with which the entire house was equipped to close against the valley's winter "wind tunnel" (Erik Kvalsvik). Opposite: Isaac Hite surveys his parlor from the wall at Belle Grove, painted by Charles Peale Polk, who also executed the portrait of his wife and son (Ping Amranand)

Above: A nineteenth-century view of Montpelier shows the house as it was expanded by the Madisons, capturing the pastoral feeling the estate had when they lived there (Library of Congress). Opposite: Even with its early twentieth-century additions to the sides, the front of Montpelier today still retains the general image into which Madison transformed it early in the nineteenth century (Robert Lautman)

The Hites' stonemasons were still constructing Belle Grove when James and Dolley Madison made their decision to keep house with his parents at Montpelier. Such arrangements were common in those days: two, even three families under one roof. Like William Henry Drayton, Madison was to be the principal heir of his parents, so his living at home made sense. At some point the transfer of power was expected to take place in the big house. It was 1797. Having cast his lot with Jefferson in opposing the Federalist Party, Madison declined the ministry to France and returned to the peace of home to await a brighter political horizon. It was at this point that a course had to be established regarding how two families would occupy Montpelier. Cohabitation was easier said than done. The elder Madisons were well along in years, but very independent, and the decision was finally made for the two households to live in entirely separate quarters, side by side. To serve this purpose, the house was enlarged.

Not for about twelve years, through two building episodes, was Montpelier to appear as James Madison, Jr., wanted it. The plan he worked out for himself. Madison was president when it was finished. By 1800, the year the federal government relocated to Washington and Thomas Jefferson beat John Adams's rebid for the presidency, one could stand on the ground before Montpelier and get a fair idea of the outline of the house we now know. The addition was made by building on the left or northeast side of the existing house, an appendage half the size of the house already there. A single door inside united the two parts, one that led from the second floor of the new wing into the small room upstairs in the old house, where the younger James Madison kept his books and office.

On the front was built a heroic-scale portico, with Tuscan columns reaching from a wooden porch to support a pediment. Like Washington's "pilastrade" porch at Mount Vernon, the portico gave the house unity and strength, while it covered up the worst of its architectural weaknesses. Now two houses in one, the mansion had unsightly scars from the process of its growth, and the plan was to coat it all with stucco, scored to look like ashlar blocks, as Benjamin Chew had done on the sides of Cliveden. When the house was occupied the cement had not been applied to the naked brick of the walls and columns for lack of a craftsman to do it, or a stucco material that suited Madison. He painted his brick. Montpelier would be just such a raw-looking country house for many years more, long after 1809, the year Madison moved to the White House. The stuccoing could wait. James and Dolley Madison, meanwhile, were seldom at Montpelier to worry over the appearance of the house. Election news in November 1800 first set them packing, to go to the new capital, where he served as secretary of state under Jefferson.

The federal city was laid out ambitiously over woods and fields and had not overcome the look of a pastoral countryside. Washington became a capital in the human sense long before the fact was realized in brick and mortar. Transplanted government people, accustomed to the city delights of

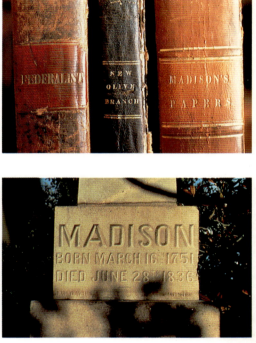

Above left: Montpelier's columned temple, built by Madison, is atop his ice house, a deep brick-lined cellar into which ice was packed layer by layer in sawdust and straw (Robert Lautman). Above right: Reminders of Madison at the property today include books such as The Federalist Papers, *in which he wrote key essays, and Madison's tombstone in the graveyard (Montpelier). Left: Dolley and James Madison owned this ordinary bamboo-style Windsor chair, which probably was painted originally (Robert Lautman). Opposite: In the mid-nineteenth century Montpelier's porch floor was cut back by later owners who removed Madison's pyramid of steps and placed the columns on plinths (Robert Lautman)*

Philadelphia, made the best of mud streets and stumps, vacant cityscapes, and cramped, costly housing, reestablishing themselves as players in the center of power. Diplomats, public employees, and elected officials hungry for settled society found it in abundance among the nearby plantation families of Maryland and Virginia. In the former there were the Carrolls, the Digges, the golden Calverts; Virginia provided the Masons, the Lees, and not least the Washingtons—or those remaining who formed the president's domestic circle at Mount Vernon.

Principal among the Washingtons were the four Custis grandchildren of Martha Washington, notably George Washington Parke Custis, called Wash, and Eleanor Parke Custis, called Nelly. The two were raised by the Washingtons on the death of their father, John Parke Custis. Had their foster grandfather become king—as heroes before him had done throughout history—and not taken the grandeur of humble retirement to his farm, these two knew full well that they would be an American prince and princess. They always acted somewhat royal, anyway, acknowledging constant reminders of their connection with the immortal Washington. Both had witnessed stirring scenes and known personally all of the great individuals of the early republic. Passing years drew them ever further from the days of Washington, so they clung ever tighter to the past glories of others. Wash liked to hunt and draw pictures. History sneers a bit at his amours with slave women and the long, pompous orations he gave over a half century in Washington on the Fourth of July. Two great associations do adorn his memory: his massive-columned Arlington House, which still overlooks the capital, and his son-in-law, Robert E. Lee.

Nelly was tall and beautiful, with the gracious manner of a queen. People admired her all of her life. As a girl she was the darling of George Washington and a youthful presence in his presidential courts in New York and Philadelphia. The Father of His Country was disappointed that she did not marry George Washington Lafayette, son of the great Lafayette, but he was delighted in 1799 when at candlelight on his birthday she married his nephew Lawrence Lewis. The nephew had once aspired to a military career and world travel, but in marrying his uncle's favorite cast his lot to stay near Mount Vernon. Washington ribbed the groom for trading the "lap of Mars" for the "sports of Venus." For a wedding present the general selected a windy hill on his lands a few miles west of Mount Vernon and attached to it 2,000 acres for a farm. Perhaps in counsel with their benefactor, Nelly and Lawrence named the farm Woodlawn.

The house was begun several years after the general's death at the close of 1799 and probably took some years to finish. Woodlawn looks toward the distant Potomac River over forest trees, a broad, tall mansion of red brick, trimmed in the same Aquia sandstone the Hites had used at Belle Grove. By family tradition, the architect was a friend, the physician William

Opposite: Woodlawn, on its lofty hill, once commanded thousands of acres devoted to grain crops, cereal, and cattle. One hundred twenty-six acres remain in forests and meadows. The trees from which the estate got its name are long since gone but have been replanted (Erik Kvalsvik)

Above: Nelly Custis and her brother Wash are shown as children with their grandmother, Martha Washington, foster father, George Washington, and one of General Washington's slaves, Billy Lee, in this famous family portrait by Edward Savage. Widely circulated as an engraving in the nineteenth century, this scene underscores the fame enjoyed by the brother and sister because of their intimate association with Washington (National Gallery of Art). Right: Woodlawn's dramatic circular staircase rises from the long hall that extends from front to back (Erik Kvalsvik). Opposite: Nelly Custis Lewis's portrait in oil above the fireplace at Woodlawn is the work of John Trumbull. The doors are painted to imitate maple, carefully duplicating the design she selected in the early nineteenth century (Ping Amranand)

Above: This upstairs bedroom at Woodlawn, with its Grecian chaise longue, is believed to have been occupied by Lafayette. The woodwork is simple, with applied ogee moldings, and is typical of other houses in the region at the time. Paint has been applied to the plaster walls, which may have been papered in some cases. Right: Across the hall is the bedroom of Nelly and Lawrence Lewis's only son, Lorenzo, whose avocation of ornithology can be seen in birds he actually mounted as well as other collections of interest to a naturalist. Nelly later went to live with Lorenzo at his farm, Audley, in the Shenandoah Valley of Virginia, only to be stunned by his early death (both, Erik Kvalsvik).

Above: The marble mantel in the music room is a later addition, using design motifs that match the French clock; both of these items and the glass chandelier came with the restoration of Woodlawn in the 1950s. Originally all three mantel ornaments— the vases and the clock—probably would have been sheltered by glass shades or domes. Left: Woodlawn's music room, on the main floor, has a portrait of Lawrence Lewis in old age, painted by John Beale Bordley, as well as objects from the period in which Nelly and Lawrence Lewis lived in the house (both, Erik Kvalsvik)

Woodlawn's garden centers in a long, broad central axis, terminated at one end by a latticed gazebo. To the sides are various planting areas, some originally for vegetables as well as flowers. The large collection of Heritage Roses here is particularly fine (Erik Kvalsvik)

Thornton, designer of the U.S. Capitol. This may or may not be so. Woodlawn is a hybrid, seemingly inspired in part by Kenmore, the childhood home of Lawrence Lewis in Fredericksburg, Virginia. Kenmore's quaint, old-fashioned pent gables mingle on the red brick pile with "Federal" neoclassicism, then the trademark of the capital.

Woodlawn's rooms are large in scale, as are the tall windows, which must have rendered the interiors chilly in winter. They admit a beautiful fall of light today, as they must have for Nelly Custis Lewis, illuminating the collections of inherited memorabilia from Mount Vernon with which she filled her rooms. The best of capital society came to call on her, especially on Sundays. Nelly and Lawrence Lewis felt it their duty to treat those they knew and those bearing letters of introduction with hospitality no less than General Washington had extended in his day. Her recipe book is filled with directions for making cakes and other sweets, as well as hints for thrifty management. Guests admired the winding stairs, and they stood on the marble floor of the columned porch to enjoy the panoramic view.

Woodlawn's building fell in an optimistic period of house construction in Virginia that took place just ahead of the general economic decline that lasted out the century. One of Nelly's friends—like her, the child of other times—built a house farther out from the capital, deep in what we know today as the Virginia hunt country, Loudoun County. George Carter was the great-grandson of Virginia's legendary Robert "King" Carter, owner of a colonial empire in land and slaves and all kinds of business endeavors. On 3,400 acres given him by his father, George Carter began his mansion, Oatlands, about 1803. The land had been in the Carter family since 1728. It was ancestral like Nelly's Woodlawn and many other Virginia estates. Virginians placed greater value than anyone on such unbroken chains.

A series of craftsmen worked on Oatlands over a long period. The roof was up in 1810, and Carter moved to his plantation from Baltimore. The house stood on a rise, although one not so sharply elevated as at Woodlawn. Originally it was a simple rectangle of red brick, a courthouse-like structure surmounted by a cupola. One could describe the original house as old-fashioned, in the same sense that Woodlawn was more a form from the past than from its own time, the past being very important to the Carters as well as the Lewises. Neither farm complex, however, was without innovation. Woodlawn had a remarkable octagonal barn, and at Oatlands the service buildings that usually surrounded southern houses were organized into terraces that stepped off down the hill to the sides, more or less out of sight. These boxy little structures, linked together, contained the laundry, offices, storage rooms, gardener's house, and the like, while the stables, barns, and farm buildings were built farther away.

A bachelor most of his life, Carter was a bright, kindly individual who increased his wealth with the Oatlands farm, taking advantage of some of the same markets that made Belle Grove and Woodlawn prosper. He was scholarly by nature and spent time away by himself reading the classics as well as current publications on husbandry, gardening, and politics. Although his father, the humanitarian "Councillor" Carter, grandson of King, divided most of his lands among his children before his death, it fell George Carter's task to manage the properties that went to his numerous sisters. They and their children imposed on the bachelor freely: "Dear Uncle George," wrote one, "you're the man of the family and there is simply no one else to whom I can apply. Mama says the crops are bad, and there'll be no gowns for the new season. I just can't face life like this."

George Carter was educated in New England, by a father whose strong moral objection to slavery made him suspicious of southern schools. When he reached middle age, Councillor Carter initiated a program of manumission of his slaves, beginning with adults over forty-five and babies as soon as they were born. The plan provided assistance to the ex-slaves in setting up a self-supporting life on their own. When the Councillor died, George Carter, although a large slaveholder himself, faithfully carried out

George Carter of Oatlands, reading the National Intelligencer, *a Republican newspaper, was almost seventy when this portrait was painted about 1844 (Wm. Edmund Barrett, Oatlands, Inc.)*

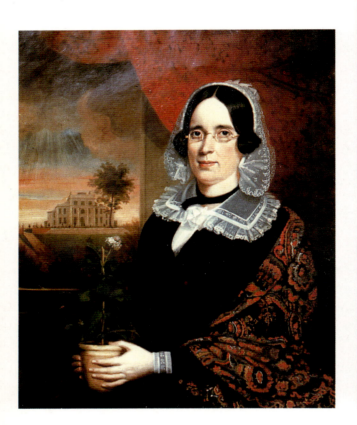

Above left: Oatlands appears in the background of this mourning portrait of Elizabeth Carter painted sometime after 1846 (Oatlands, Inc.). Above right: Her sons Benjamin and George Carter were painted with a noble companion about 1848 (Oatlands, Inc.). Right: The view out from the house captures the portico's ornate Corinthian column capitals that George Carter commissioned in New York (Erik Kvalsvik). Opposite: Divided from the house by a balustrade, the terraced gardens have been restored and present an array of flowering plants and old boxwood hedges (Ping Amranand)

Above: Although almost two centuries old, Oatlands has been owned by only two families, the Carters and the Eustises. The richly architectural entrance hall is seen here as it was in the Eustis years, with the stately portraits of William Eustis's parents, George and Louise Corcoran Eustis, painted in Rome in 1859 (Erik Kvalsvik). Left: Isabel Hill McCalla's 1888 watercolor shows the hall as the Carters, the original owners, had it, with their family portraits, large Greek Revival furniture, hunt trophies, and comfortable chairs (Oatlands, Inc.). Opposite: The drawing room today has furnishings added by the Eustis family in the early twentieth century (Ping Amranand)

his father's wishes, even though he realized that the courts would have readily authorized him to discontinue the program. He honored his father's sensitivities on slavery but kept his own slaves in bondage, some seventy-five of all ages by the 1820s. At that time many Virginia planters were fighting the falling economy by selling off slaves to traders who took them down south to the cotton and cane fields. Carter took no part; he appears, however, to have increased his need for workers through a constant series of new agricultural projects. For all of his agrarian experimentation and modern farming and milling endeavors, Carter felt the bite of hard times practically every year.

He can be described if not as a frugal or tight man, certainly as one who made sure where his money was and what it was doing. The economic storms that blew against Virginia for so many years did not send him under, which made it possible for him to indulge his interest in architecture and kept him adding to his house well into the 1830s. The presence of so much building in the federal city, and the neoclassical models offered there, spawned a whole generation of carpenters and plasterers and other tradesmen who, with the help of plan books, executed work in that style. Already by the time of the 1812 war with England, Carter had begun to embellish Oatlands with sumptuous neoclassical plasterwork. The additions represented an odd combination of the stylish and the archaic. Eventually, the house was given semioctagonal projections at each end, to house curving stairs, and on the front a florid Corinthian portico rising the full two stories over a high base. The wooden column capitals were commissioned from Henry Farnham, carver of New York City.

Countryman that he was, George Carter naturally loved the out-of-doors. He gardened at Oatlands, producing fine fruits and vegetables. Wild game and fish he brought in for the sport of it. His horses and hounds were the finest in the county, and his neighbor James Monroe's diplomatic guests sometimes came to hunt with him. Mounted hunts among the Virginians were tough and sometimes dangerous cross-country adventures through field and stream, the participants' daring fueled with whiskey or rum taken in large quantities. The great season for horseback hunting was fall, when the crops were in, but the country people hunted all year.

George Carter took some interest in female company, and as a man of fifty-nine he took a wife, Elizabeth O. Lewis, widow of an old hunting companion. A devoted gardener and lover of country life, Elizabeth proudly described herself, writing her own epitaph, as "a lady seldom, if ever, erring from her first judgement." A portrait of her shows a perky country dame, holding a flower pot with one of her fine specimens. She organized the ex-bachelor's life to such an extent that his last ten years were not as peaceful as the many that had gone before. Two sons were born, to carry on at Oatlands, until the chain of the old Virginia land title was at last broken in the late nineteenth century. For the time being, the Carters were securely among the Old Dominion's gentry, which by the nineteenth century was already pleased to describe itself as a reflection of the English aristocracy.

Stephen and Susan Decatur's house, pictured in this watercolor by a neighbor, Madame E. Vaile, about 1822, occupied a prominent position on the square across from the White House. Because of this location, it was home to a succession of distinguished persons (Gordon Beall, Decatur House)

From time to time George Carter joined the Lewises, Custises, and other Virginia clans in political society during Washington's social season, which opened with the first White House dinner in December and closed with the last in April or May, depending on the weather. This association was interesting not only for the presence of the political celebrities of the day, but also for the dash of spice provided by the diplomats from abroad. Country families joined house parties with town cousins and got on the lists for dinners and balls both through friendships and on the authority of their old family names. Capital society had little splendor in the years before the War of 1812, but after Washington was burned two years later and rebuilt, and in full operation by 1818, it was clearly recognized for its liberality, gaiety, strictness of form, and, as in any capital, networks of power, prestige, and personal advancement.

Among those attracted to the national capital to try high ambitions in public life was Commodore Stephen Decatur, hero of the Tripoli War and already one of the most popular men in the United States. He had the profile of Alexander and pronounced masculine grace; the man seemed to take leadership for granted. His star-spangled naval career shone with daring adventures and distinguished achievements. That one day this godlike individual might be president in the White House was more than obvious to many, not least to himself, or his pretty wife, Susan. Stationed in Washington in peacetime, the Decaturs determined to establish themselves very publicly.

In 1818, when the president's catch phrase for the new age, the "era of good feelings," was on everyone's lips, the Decaturs met with Benjamin Henry Latrobe about building a fine house. Latrobe, born in England to

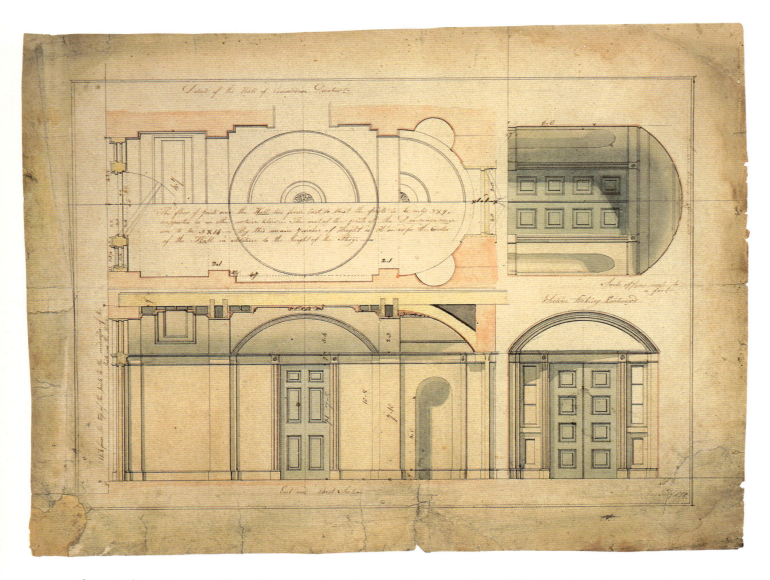

Above: Architect Benjamin Henry Latrobe's drawings for the entrance hall at Decatur House detailed vaults that made a dramatic effect in a house that presented a plain exterior to the street (Library of Congress). Opposite: The entrance hall now provides access to a north room, through a door cut many years after Decatur's time. This room is generally believed to be the one in which Decatur died after his duel with James Barron. On the wall is a portrait of Decatur's brother, Colonel John Paine Decatur (Ping Amranand)

an American mother, was well established in America as an architect whose practice had taken him from Philadelphia and Pittsburgh to Washington. He was the best of the country's early architects and is often called the first professional architect in America, although it is safer to say that he was among the first. His genius had come to public acclaim in the templelike neoclassical splendor of Philadelphia's Bank of Pennsylvania and the old House of Representatives in the U.S. Capitol. An ardent republican, he was inspired to eloquence by freedom's architectural challenges. The Decaturs took him to their lot on the corner of H Street, at the head of the President's Park, overlooking the grassy public common and in full view of that freshly rebuilt Aquia stone pile, the White House. He agreed to give them a house of the modern sort.

The fine red brick town house that has come down in history as Decatur House was built between 1818 and 1819. Exactly what Stephen and Susan Decatur required in a house is uncertain. Given the probability that the commodore might move away for extended periods, as he always had, they wanted the option of renting the house to foreign ministers, perhaps retaining part of the ground floor or some other area for their temporary

harbor. The architect designed the house in a mode he had made his own in America, the English classic "Plain Style," a version of neoclassicism that emphasized classical form and proportions more than decorative detailing. It was a reaction to the more frothy historical representations of the Adam brothers and their generation of British architects. Latrobe's simple monumentality recalled the work of Sir John Soane in England. At Decatur House the essay is in red brick and very restrained wood trim, with slight touches of stone in steps and lintels. It is a tall block of a house placed firmly against the corner, with deep eaves all around like a Tuscan farmhouse. From outside the shapes of the windows denote a low ground floor, a tall second or main floor—to Latrobe the first floor—and a lower ceiling on the top floor.

The building opens into an entrance hall where the classical motif is clarified in bands of pilasters and groin vaulting simulated in plaster on wood lath to resemble stone construction. Rooms opened only off the south side of this hall; beyond the solid wall on the north side Latrobe planned service rooms entered elsewhere, perhaps even a kitchen, which Decatur used as an office. In a second hall beyond the entrance hall the sharply rising, curving stair swept to gala rooms on the second or main floor. Here was the drawing room, with a small room behind it, perhaps a fancy bedchamber. A large dining room was climaxed by a half-circle alcove containing a sideboard, flanked by small doors into the service area. Bedchambers occupied the third floor.

In this house the Decaturs' climb to power was dramatized in rich dinners and fine wines, the glow of candles and Argand lamps, the sheen of French-polished mahogany, silks, and silver. The Decaturs lost no time in opening their house to those they wished to cultivate: senators, congressmen, officers of the military, foreign ministers, and not least the president of the United States. Somehow Decatur seemed to represent the navy at its most heroic. Washington society was young, rather frisky by the standards of more staid urban society, but the interactions and competition among its members were close at hand and could be vicious. The company often was gay and candid. Women mixed freely in the conversations of men. Caterers of French and Belgian extraction made good livings in the season, supplying sumptuous food—always French—to such dinners as Commodore Decatur held, and navy ships reporting home could be depended on to produce a cache of cases and barrels of wines and liquors. The falsetto-voiced orator John Randolph of Roanoke praised the fine Bordeaux Susan Decatur brought up from her cellar. In her pantry she stored more than a hundred wine glasses and seventeen decanters.

It is universal that immoderate ambition can be a dangerous business. Close to the fire of power, the commodore made his enemies. He was a man with an unsavory, violent side known to very few people. Rivalries breed insults, and honor makes its demands. In Washington at Christmas 1818 appeared an old navy friend and companion officer of Decatur, Commodore James Barron, ending a decade of heartbroken wandering in Europe.

Above: Susan Decatur's portrait was painted in 1802 by Gilbert Stuart and his assistants (Gordon Beall, Decatur House). Opposite: After he achieved fame, naval hero Stephen Decatur was depicted in many popular portraits such as this one by Alonzo Chappel (Library of Congress)

Humiliated by the navy for his inept command of the *Chesapeake* back in Jefferson's administration, his suspension had passed and he was anxious to reinstate himself. He appeared, standing straight, looking for friends among those who had accused him, including Decatur. Tale carriers taunted Barron with sarcastic remarks. Soon Decatur's name was attached to the barbs. A threatening correspondence ensued, then the inevitable challenge. Unknown to his wife, a hesitant Decatur left his house before day on March 22, 1820, and faced Barron in the Maryland countryside, just as the sun was appearing. Stephen Decatur was brought home to die.

Susan Decatur grieved in dark rooms and recalled to everyone who would listen how in her fourteen years of marriage her husband had "strewed my daily path with flowers! and never caused me a moment's pain save that which sprung from my unbounded affection and anxiety for his preservation!" But all that had glittered for them had not been paid for, and at last the realities of little cash drove her into the light of day. Eventual conversion to Roman Catholicism twenty years later soothed her pain. Meanwhile, Susan held a public sale of her furnishings (which Mrs. Barron attended) and moved out, renting her house to produce income. She and the commodore had cast a spell over the place. The motives that caused them to create it would reappear again and again in other minds and other ambitions within the house, and always the distant, sad memory of the first dreamers cut down hovered, at once a benediction and a warning.

As the half-century anniversary of the Declaration of Independence approached, a grateful American people invited the aging Marquis de Lafayette to come be their guest for a sentimental journey to the United States. This invitation was grandly accepted, and a battleship transported the Hero of Two Worlds, with his son George Washington Lafayette, servants, and the general's companion, the writer Fanny Wright. She idolized Lafayette and had discreetly added her sister Camilla to the party as chaperone.

What a splendid man Lafayette was! No longer the slim youth who had fought with Washington, he had grown mellow and stately. His history had been followed by Americans with avid interest for more than forty years, tracing his political and military adventures in the French Revolution, imprisonment in Austria, and participation in successive governments in France. Arriving in New York on Sunday, August 15, 1824, he was surrounded by ships in the harbor and thousands of spectators on shore. General William Paulding, mayor of New York, informed him, however, that they must not mar the Sabbath with a great public display. Lafayette waited and swept ashore on Monday. America was his.

The party went practically everywhere for a year, accepting banquets and orations in Lafayette's praise. He went to the White House, the first guest of state to stay there, and President Monroe ordered the new park cut out of the common in front of the house named Lafayette Square. In the course of his stay at Monticello, the glorious guest went to visit the Madisons at Montpelier. Madison was writing his history of the Constitutional Convention in his library above the front door. A turbaned, rouged Dolley showed Lafayette her French salon, a long crowded drawing room that extended down the center of the house, its furniture and hangings gilded and primped, the walls lined with busts and pictures of men who, with her husband, had molded the United States from colonial clay. Near the end of the tour he visited Cliveden, site of the 1777 Battle of Germantown, where a crowd heard him review his memories of the fighting there, but for which, he believed, the American Revolution might have ended sooner.

Everywhere the crowds were big and joyous, tears mixed generously with the huzzahs. Old vets came out by the hundreds. Triumphal arches greeted the hero, and parades escorted him through them. That he was on hard times was quietly known, and many of the legislative bodies in the newer states made grants of land to him. He was eloquent in his gratitude, but of all the events that touched the general, his visit to his old friends at Woodlawn seems to have warmed him the most. Here he and his son visited twice, remaining several days with Nelly Custis Lewis, whom Lafayette had never met but regarded as blood kin. Nelly lost no time in hurrying Fanny and Camilla on their way, even though the general assured her that the relationship was not a romance. She wanted her friends for herself. Their days would be spent in joyous conversations. Old times would live again.

At Woodlawn the pace of the American tour slowed, away from the trumpets and drums. As a boy, George Washington Lafayette had lived with the Washingtons for several years following his escape from the revolution in France. When he was able to return to France he did so, over the affectionate protests of his protector, who had hoped he and Nelly would marry and found an American dynasty. George and Nelly laughed now as they had then over Washington's efforts to play Cupid. By 1824 both had families. They called each other "brother" and "sister" and heard the Marquis de Lafayette tell his stories of General Washington, his "father."

The visit, iridescent in the chronicles of Woodlawn, evokes more than it tells us in fact. These three lives, lived for the most part separately, had been drawn together over time by great events and characters. Their combined experiences included revolutions in America and France, achievement, joy, disappointment, tragedy; hard realities survived in the frustrated ambition of Nelly to be more than she was, and of the Frenchman to wear the laurels of a tumultuous age. An old drawing that hangs on the wall at Woodlawn captures the moment, showing them together on the steep hill that still seems to float above the stars, three symbols of an epoch in time gone by.

The visit of the Lewises and the Lafayettes at Woodlawn in 1824 was commemorated by John Robert Murray (Woodlawn)

A. Persac. 1861.

Age of Enterprise

America awakened to itself as a nation after the War of 1812. From that event, and for a long time afterward, it was increasingly shaped by the rise of the West. Even as Lafayette and Nelly Custis Lewis contemplated history on Woodlawn's hill, the nation was readjusting practically everywhere, trying to ignore its own contradictions, but never stopping to breathe much in its lust to grasp opportunity—in farming, in invention, in the swelling new phenomenon of the marketplace. The magnet of the unclaimed West was a great force in life. Jefferson's purchase of the Louisiana Territory had its most dramatic results only after the War of 1812 freed the Mississippi River for commerce between the sea and America's backwoods. A significant part of the American population began to shift into the new regions.

The growing pains were terrible for some. When Andrew Jackson's election in 1828 confirmed the idea that the common people were at last to take their rightful place in the democracy, the old order seemed to crumble. In rented Decatur House, Henry Clay, the outgoing secretary of state, threw himself on the drawing room sofa and wept, pondering his political ruin. He soon

Opposite: Gothic architectural detailing at Lyndhurst, General William Paulding's manor above the Hudson River, is theatrical and complete. This transverse corridor shows the original entrance hall, with its floors of marble tiles and plaster walls painted to imitate Siena marble. In Paulding's day the long corridor ended at a stairhall; this view includes later additions on beyond. The busts of George Washington and Lafayette, owned by Paulding, have never left the house (Gordon Beall)

❧

Preceding pages: In 1861 artist Adrien Persac painted this detailed record of the Shadows on Bayou Teche, one of two egg tempera paintings that show the Louisiana house on both its waterfront and town sides when the Weeks family resided there (Shadows-on-the-Teche)

parted to make way for a new tenant, Martin Van Buren of New York, secretary of state to Jackson. The new president was inaugurated, amid joyous crowds, but he was in deep mourning for his wife, Rachel; he insisted that her death was hastened by slander. Feeble and in poor health, Jackson exerted little leadership, so those surrounding him struggled to take control. Political Washington fell into a period of turmoil. Lines that had seemed so clearly drawn were blurred now to confusion that extended even to the drawing room, as rivalries surfaced among people who had pulled together for Jackson, so short a time before.

The inevitable explosion came at the point of least resistance: society. At one of Van Buren's dinners at Decatur House, early in the administration, Andrew Jackson was angered over the snubbing of the wife of a member of his political family; the presence of Peggy O'Neale Eaton, new wife of John Eaton, secretary of war, had kept away most of the other women. This was the culmination of a situation that had annoyed Jackson, who soon took up her defense. Few people would proclaim with a straight face that Peggy Eaton's reputation was unblemished, but Jackson heard in the treatment of her echoes of the slanders that had been hurled at Mrs. Jackson. By entering the fray the president gave it undue attention, so that it became the first major event of his administration, remembered as the "petticoat war." Peggy Eaton was determined to storm into the leading role in society; to thwart her victory, the cabinet wives, and the women of Jackson's own household, united in declining invitations to events where she was sure to be present. For this reason women were sparsely represented at Van Buren's dinner. An immovable Jackson eventually lost, after long months of controversy. But the battle was the catalyst for the president's cabinet to resign one by one, except for the widower Van Buren, whose single status saved him. He emerged from the wreckage a man with bright prospects, firmly on the road to the presidency. More than ever he meticulously cultivated his rip-snorting patron. Still visible at Decatur House are traces of a window that Van Buren ordered cut in the blank south wall upstairs, so he could receive mirror signals night and day to hurry over to the White House and serve Old Hickory.

The next renter of Decatur House, following what had become an informal tradition, was Van Buren's successor as secretary of state, Edward Livingston. A much-respected legal scholar and senior statesman, he left New York, where his family had come to dominate politics, and made a career in Louisiana. He was reluctant to take on the duties of the State Department at the age of sixty-seven but accepted President Jackson's offer. Society was part of the job, and Livingston's household was graced by his second wife, Marie Louisa d'Avezac Castra Moreau, a radiant Creole who thirty years before had fled with her family to New Orleans from the slave rebellion in Santa Domingo. The character of Livingston's entertainments was described by one of his better-known guests, Gustave de Beaumont, who, with his more famous traveling companion, Alexis de Tocqueville, spent several evenings at Decatur House in January 1832, having just con-

Martin Van Buren rented Decatur House while serving in Andrew Jackson's first cabinet, before he himself became president (Library of Congress)

cluded their long travels in the interior of the continent. Beaumont found that Livingston spoke French "wonderfully well" and was "almost French in his ways." The soirée was charming but the music bad. The concert did not last long, however, and soon, he wrote to an American friend, the guests began to dance. "I mingled my square dances and waltzes with most interesting conversations with Mr. Livingston on the penitentiary system and especially on capital punishment. . . . "

With the Livingstons' departure in 1833, the British minister to Washington, Sir Richard Charles Vaughan, moved in to Decatur House, breaking its tradition as the unofficial residence of the secretary of state. Entertainments nonetheless continued in the best Washington style. But after Vaughan the mansion on Lafayette Square was less remarkable until just before the Civil War, when several southerners rented it, notably another Louisiana couple.

I n the aftermath of Jackson's greatest political struggle, the bank wars of the 1830s, the financial heart of the nation shifted largely from Philadelphia to New York. Manhattan in the 1830s had rivals only in Philadelphia and New Orleans and outstripped all other American cities as a great metropolis. Architectural remains from this time are few—some churches and houses, the old city hall. Nineteenth-century New York life survives more provocatively in the country houses its rich citizens built during these years up the Hudson River, in the swelling hills and forests of the old Dutch counties. This beautiful region was much in the popular imagination from the 1820s to the 1870s, in literature and in art from the Hudson River School of landscape painters. Mansions began to rise along the river, built by city businessmen imitating to an extent their English counterparts in London, Liverpool, and Manchester, who enjoyed living part time in the country and working in town.

One of the greatest houses of the Hudson is Lyndhurst, built in an imposing Gothic castle style near Tarrytown. In its youth, this area was only a couple of hours by steamboat from Manhattan. The lofty marble pile would have pleased a banker or a poet alike, in the sublime silhouette it cast against the horizon. From its castle towers the panorama of the Hudson River—the Tappan Zee, Haverstraw Bay—spreads in both directions through green hills. It began as a smaller house called the Knoll, or perhaps just Knoll.

General William Paulding, the mayor of New York whose religious scruples had delayed Lafayette's entrance into the city, was born six years before the Declaration of Independence and was sixty-eight when he and his bachelor son, Philip, decided in about 1838 to build a country house. He had acquired an old Dutch farm in the region of his birth, where his own distinguished family dated back a century, first as tenants, then as landholders themselves. Returning so grandly was not without its triumph. William Paulding remembered a painful boyhood, when his father—hero

General William Paulding, builder of Lyndhurst, was painted by Samuel F. B. Morse in 1826 (City Hall Collection, City of New York)

to his sons—was in debtors prison and he and his brother James took him his meals, suffering through Tarrytown's streets the mockery of other children. Through William and James, who became the well-known wit and poet James Kirke Paulding, the Pauldings could stand proud again. In a long career as a lawyer, William Paulding built a fortune. He missed home. After his service in the War of 1812, when he rose to the rank of brigadier general, he spent vacation time in various Hudson River towns, but his work was in Manhattan, where he was a leading citizen and an ardent Jacksonian Democrat. Philip Paulding may have had to persuade his father to build a fine house on his land on the Hudson, for General Paulding was neither ambitious in that way nor young enough to take on the task. Eager to retire, he turned over most of the development of the estate to his son.

Paulding's property, consisting of about a hundred acres, was in walking distance of Sunnyside, the residence of the celebrated author Washington Irving. They were kin, Irving's brother being married to Paulding's sister, but Irving was also a long-time friend of Paulding's brother, the poet James. Irving has been called America's Sir Walter Scott, and as Scott had lived in an Ivanhoe castle, Abbotsford, Irving had gone to live among the scenes of his famous Knickerbocker characters and built himself a "Dutch" house. The Pauldings also sought a historical motif in their new house, but they took their cue from Scott, not Irving.

To design the new house, General Paulding and Philip in 1838 engaged architect A. J. Davis. He was a young practitioner in New York, partner of the better-known architect and bridge builder Ithiel Town, with whom William Paulding had been acquainted. Davis was becoming known for his work in the Grecian and Gothic styles. The handsome drawings he produced projected an asymmetrical villa of superb brick construction faced in stone, Gothic style, but with generous porches and large windows that were more those of a church or college than a castle. It was at once cottage and castle, certainly a home to which Paulding might go for a dignified retirement.

The exterior stone was Sing-Sing marble, superbly dressed in ashlar blocks and carved into Gothic moldings with as much refinement as if it had been intended for use on a public building. On the inside where stone stopped and plaster began, the richer materials were imitated in painted striations that resembled marble as well as gray paint thickened with sand that gave the wood a sandstone look. The interior spaces formed a succession of vaulted Gothic-style rooms made to look like masonry construction, a deceit carried out in plaster over lath, like Latrobe's groined hall at Decatur House. From a deep porte-cochère, one passed through a series of squarish spaces, terminating in a large reception room with rippled Gothic windows facing the river. A transverse axis crossed the room about center point, led to a large drawing room to the left, and passed between the dining room and the office on the right, terminating in a stairhall. For such a house Paulding's was relatively small, but its public rooms were ample and highly dramatic, with pointed vaults and colors of purple and ruby and the

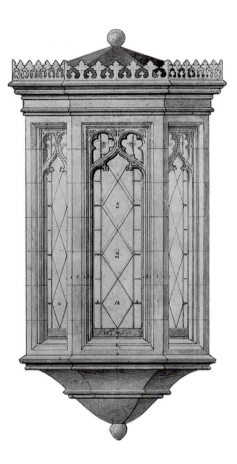

Above: Architect A. J. Davis not only designed the castle that Paulding wanted, he also returned a quarter century later and made additions so sensitive to the original that new and old seemed the same. Davis's drawing for an oriel window in the great tower was realized in the addition (Harris Brisbane Dick Fund, Metropolitan Museum of Art). Opposite: Lyndhurst's Gothic outline against the sky imparts the theatrical flavor of romantic nineteenth-century architecture (Gordon Beall)

Above: A. J. Davis's drawing for the expansion of Lyndhurst in the Civil War period shows the Knoll house extended with a great wing and towers. Right: The 1838 villa became the core of the house that was much enlarged by Davis in 1864–1865 (both, Harris Brisbane Dick Fund, Metropolitan Museum of Art)

rich yellow of Siena marble. The interior climaxed on the second floor, in a great mead hall of a library projecting beyond the center of the house, its plaster corbels cast with the faces of famous authors and historical figures. Tall windows welcomed a panoramic view of the Hudson River from the lofty knoll.

Construction ran on from late 1839 until about 1842. The younger Paulding and Davis corresponded with some frequency. Philip Paulding called at workshops and furniture warehouses in New York, making selections appropriate for the new house. When the market yielded too little in the Gothic style, which had become a mania with him, Davis was commissioned to design special furniture for the house. His more than fifty pieces took motifs from Gothic architecture, the chairs both tall with Gothic-arch backs and low with backs shaped like the rose windows in a cathedral. The beds had massive headboards, like church reredos.

Life on the Hudson with this class of people still involved New York rather intimately. Steamboats ran between the city and the various towns along the river. The Pauldings set up residence at the villa, but they were often in Manhattan. They must have pressed to the steamboat's rail for a first sight of their marble house on its hill: the tall chimneys, the pointed gable, the diamond-paned windows. One commuter drove by land to see "Mr. Paulding's magnificent house" in 1842: "It is an immense edifice of

Lyndhurst, seen here from the riverbank at sunset, always had a special relationship to the Hudson River. From their rural retreat, the Pauldings commuted to the city by steamboat. Later owner Jay Gould also traveled by river on his own yacht (Gordon Beall)

91

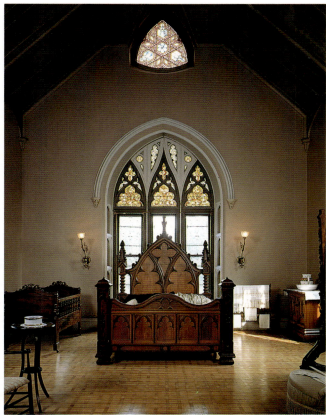

Top: The new dining room was added in the 1865 expansion of Lyndhurst (Jim Frank). Left: A second-floor bedroom has appropriately Gothic furniture (Gordon Beall). Above: The room Paulding used as a library was converted in 1865 into a billiard room and art gallery. Open-flame gas chandeliers lighted the tall space, and both pictures and louvered blinds masked the spectacular view of the Hudson from the Gothic window (Lyndhurst). Opposite: In a later remodeling, the library's window was uncovered (Gordon Beall)

white or gray marble, resembling a baronial castle, or rather a Gothic monastery, with towers, turrets and trellises; archways, armoires, and air-holes; peaked windows and pinnacled roofs, and many other fantastics." Paulding's home became and remains one of the most handsome architectural landmarks along the Hudson, among the finest of Davis's buildings and the best to endure.

Guests wandered in the summer along the river's edge, and in winter they enjoyed being within, warmed by coal fires. The villa was a romantic setting for entertaining, and hospitality among the estates on the Hudson was well known. Fashionable dinners in those days in the country still began at the quaint old-fashioned time of about four in the afternoon and ran on at table sometimes until eight or later, with course after course, climaxed by port wine and perhaps, with an old gentleman like the elder Paulding, a toast or two (although toasting at private dinners in the city was by now déclassé). Paulding's friends included patroons, prominent businessmen, politicians, and celebrities such as former President Van Buren. Many prominent New Yorkers enjoyed the abundance of the Paulding home. Now and then the sage of Sunnyside called with his beloved nieces, over whom he was a mother hen. The bachelor Irving had laid his domestic hearth before them to enjoy, and they returned his devotion. One of these girls caught the eye of Philip Paulding, and for a while Irving rejoiced at the prospect of so rich a marriage for the dear one. A proposal was made, then withdrawn. Irving's annoyance over this knew no bounds. In a letter he referred icily to current gossip about Paulding's "manor," but he assured his correspondent that no "manners" were to be found there.

The 1830s more readily call to mind America's expansion west than the good life along the Hudson. There were several Wests: the old Southwest of Andrew Jackson and Henry Clay; the old Northwest we call the Midwest; the Northwest of Lewis and Clark; what we call the Deep South, also once a "West"; and the Far or Spanish West, beyond the borders of the United States as it then was.

The mania for land investment in the Mississippi Valley attracted legions of settlers overland early in the nineteenth century and fewer perhaps by river and sea. Some — a very few — from the United States ventured as far away as Spanish California. These regions were unlike the somnolent wilderness woods Daniel Boone first entered or James Fenimore Cooper and Washington Irving wrote about, for when Americans got there, the Indians had already yielded to a greater or lesser degree to European settlement, which, if it seemed scattered on a map, was nonetheless dominant.

The frontiers of Louisiana and California produced three new houses, ones that borrowed more from the land than the houses already encountered in this book. The Shadows-on-the-Teche in Louisiana, an Anglo-American bastion in the French-speaking bayou country, was built all at once, while

the other two—Casa Amesti and the Cooper-Molera Adobe, originally the Cooper House—evolved over time, products of California's political changes, as the culture around them was altered from Latin American to Anglo-American.

Westward settlement was accelerated by victory in the 1812–1815 war with England. The idea of what was "West" seemed to move ever farther toward the sunset. One family bound from one of the old colonial states to new ground in Louisiana was the Conrads. They may have passed the rising walls of the Hites' Belle Grove as they departed Winchester overland, through the valley of Virginia. They settled on low, flat plantation lands along the Mississippi River in Louisiana, near New Orleans, where a long-established French-speaking culture thrived. One by one the Conrad children grew up and married. On the last day of 1818 Mary Clara, a Conrad daughter, married David Weeks of West Feliciana Parish, upriver. One of Mary Clara's brothers, Charles, was to bring home a bride from Virginia: Angela, daughter of Nelly and Lawrence Lewis of Woodlawn; they lived in or near New Orleans for the relatively few years they had together.

The Weekses left the cotton fields in Feliciana for higher stakes in south Louisiana sugar cane, in which the state was experiencing a boom

Adrien Persac's painting of the town front of the Shadows was made in 1861 from the yard across the street. As with the view from Bayou Teche (pages 82–83), Persac has shown scientific attention to detail. The trees appear to have been planted and pruned to remain alike (Shadows-on-the-Teche)

The lower gallery of the Shadows accommodated the stairs to the living spaces on the second floor. The only formal space on the ground floor was the dining room, which opens on this gallery and a rear loggia (© Philip Gould)

that was to last nearly to the end of the century. Their first sugar land was on the island of Grand Côte in the Attakapas country, so called after its native inhabitants, who were still much in evidence. By the seventh year of their marriage, prosperity led them to additional investments on Bayou Teche, a navigable stream that flowed through one of the richest farming regions in the nation, the parishes south of Baton Rouge, toward the Gulf of Mexico. Sugar plantations hugged the banks of the Teche as it wound through a semitropical landscape dense in foliage, one distinguished by the great oak trees and their Spanish moss. In 1825 David and Mary Clara Weeks purchased a tract of land on the Teche near the town of New Iberia and began building a house. With its tall Tuscan columns across the front, and dormer windows high above, it was to be known in later years of fame as the Shadows-on-the-Teche.

It was an odd house for its location. Wisely, the planners adopted tried measures to make it yield to the fierce Louisiana climate. The house had a deep porch, and in the tradition of the Gulf crescent and the Caribbean, it had no halls, only a shallow line of rooms linked together, with their windows and doors placed to allow for cross-ventilation when open or shielded by louvered shutters. In their scale, the rooms had the Louisiana charm of restraint, without the barnlike overscale common to nearly all large houses elsewhere in the South. The main living space was in the center, upstairs, in

the path of the Gulf breeze, above the mildew. Ample *galeries* provided open-air sitting rooms. Otherwise the Weeks mansion bore little resemblance to the Louisiana model, which was characterized by porch-shaded second-floor living quarters made entirely of wood, mounted atop a fully visible basement of brick below, for service and storage. The plan of the Shadows, however, was somewhat the same and the manner of use also very similar, but the Weeks house looked different from the outside, and it was wholly Anglo-American in its woodwork and other detailing within.

David Weeks worked hard, continuing to accumulate land and slaves and making money from sugar, some cotton, and sweet potatoes, for which the region—Cajun Louisiana—is famous today. Mary Clara was more a business partner to her husband than was usual in marriages of the time, and this arrangement found favor from a woman's point of view in the unique Louisiana legal system, which was and still is based on French law and not English precedent. A large amount of the property was kept in her name. The brick walls of the Shadows were probably completed and its brick colonnade plastered in 1834 when David Weeks went east for medical treatment.

He was scared about his business affairs, particularly his debts, for although the booming economy was still good, there were signs of deterioration. Fear for David Weeks had turned into what we would call

The rear loggia of the Shadows looks out over the lawn to Bayou Teche and a more recent garden house. The Persac painting (pages 82–83) shows that this loggia was already enclosed by the time of the Civil War (© Philip Gould)

97

depression but they called melancholy or "the glooms." Mary Clara, alarmed, tried to soothe him in a letter. She had spoken of his debts to a neighboring businessman, who was very encouraging. "[Y]ou know he is a good Authority—I only mention this to convince you that you take a wrong view of your affairs. . . . Mr. P and S think there is but few planters as free from embarrassment as you are—." Then good news about the house: "[O]ur old furniture distributed about the rooms looks better than you would think—we have got from New Orleans one dozen thirteen dollar chairs that I have put in the dineing room. . . . I want you my beloved David to make us perfectly happy—you with us in better health—I should be the happiest mortal the world contains—O my dearest Husband it is impossible to express half the affection I feel for you—O my God that I was with you—that I could rest my acheing head & heart on that dear bosom that is dearer to me than all else in this world."

Word of his death in New Haven preceded the arrival of crates of furniture he had bought for the new house. She had told him not to spend money on her, that she would make do. Some of these gifts of the melancholy husband can be seen in the Shadows today. Mary Clara Weeks stayed on, and her heirs would stay. Shrewd in business, she was wary that she might be taken in by unscrupulous overseers or sugar factors or

Above: The parlor on the second floor was the grandest room in the house and contains the portrait of Alfred Weeks, a son of the original owners (© Philip Gould). Opposite: This bedroom, restored to the period of Mary Clara Weeks, shows original furnishings and toys. The bed, rather than the window, is draped in mosquito netting to screen it against insects (Ping Amranand)

bankers. Vehement in her dislike of Roman Catholics, she did not trust her French-speaking neighbors, Creole or Cajun. She pulled her family close around her, children and blacks, and was braced against the world. She employed a tutor, a Yale graduate named Hiram Stetson, and the six children learned their lessons at home.

She did not always seclude herself like a hermit. New Orleans was a day away, with its restaurants and French and American operas. Brother Charles and Angela were there. Now and then she indulged herself. Eventually Mary Clara married again. Perhaps she saw in Judge John Moore a protector for the future, but she was cautious: a marriage contract made on April 15, 1841, the day they married, assured a strict distinction between their possessions. The Moores were a congenial couple. She continued to do much of her own business; he was interested less in his legal practice than in politics. His own plantations elsewhere in Louisiana provided sufficient income, and he was able to pursue public office. Moore, therefore, was often away. Mary Clara operated a small farm at the Shadows, which was essentially a town property, but she sent enough to market to cover most of her domestic expenses. The family plantations, from which the Weeks income came, were distant from town, one on an island. As soon as he was old enough, a son took over these.

Mary Clara referred to her Woodlawn kin-in-marriage as "aristocrats," apparently with a touch of apology for their airs. Angela Lewis Conrad's sister Parke married George Francis Butler, of a prominent Louisiana family, and moved to a plantation near St. Francisville. Now and then Nelly came to spend some time with them, but although she and Lawrence Lewis were experiencing some hard times at Woodlawn, they were unwilling to move west. Whether they ever went to the Shadows is not known, but probably not, and if so, not very pleasantly, because in later years they were rather chilly when John Moore, in Congress in Washington, made a family call. Angela was pregnant in 1839 when she became ill. Charles took her to Pass Christian on the Gulf Coast in Mississippi, with the idea that the salt air would revive her. The child was born there, but Angela did not improve and died in September. A distraught Charles Conrad and the Lewises comforted one another in long letters. Angela's remains were kept in Louisiana until 1843, when they were moved to Mount Vernon to lie in the golden orbit of the Father of His Country, where Nelly herself would one day finally rest.

Mary Clara Weeks survived her husband, David, and remarried a judge and Congressman, John Moore. She was married to Judge Moore when this portrait was made by John Beale Bordley, who also painted members of the related Lewis family at Woodlawn (Gordon Beall, Shadows-on-the-Teche)

Times were hard in Virginia in the 1830s, and the national panic in 1837 was a terrible blow to an already dying economy. At Montpelier James Madison, eighty-five, died on June 26, 1836. The world had come to call on him in his last years, often with questions about what the founders had meant by this or that in the Constitution, for the Constitution was being questioned stridently every day and in a mere quarter century would stand the ultimate test of survival. Old and withered, Madison, still sharp of mind, answered the questions with patience. Dolley stood always at his side, grown heavy but ever chipper; she held to her youth with heavy rouge and false hair, reaping the usual results of such efforts but still never failing to charm all those who met her.

After Madison's death, Dolley Madison worried that she could not manage Montpelier alone. It was not making much money, being affected by Virginia's lamentable economic situation, although it supported her immediate needs. Her son, Payne Todd, who had hovered from afar while Madison was alive, now circled on his mother like a buzzard. To pay his debts, she began to mortgage her land. At last, desperate to raise cash, she sold part of Montpelier in 1842 and the rest two years later. The cash was gone soon enough, but, meanwhile, she returned to Washington, the scene of her former glory, making her home in her sister's house across Lafayette Square from Decatur House. She could easily walk one block to White House events from there (but always, however, accepted the president's standing offer of his coach and four). Her money an alcoholic Payne threw away at gambling, whoring, and wild business and building schemes. As a means of helping her, Henry Clay and Daniel Webster persuaded Congress to purchase Madison's constitutional papers for a handsome $25,000, the same as the annual salary of the president. But this money, which could have relieved his mother's financial worries, Payne soon had in his hands, and it too was gone. She never complained of his torments, nor would she listen to others who counseled her against him. In her eyes, the tragedy of Payne Todd was probably of her making.

Lawrence Lewis died later in the same autumn of his daughter Angela's death, 1839, and after seven years Nelly put Woodlawn on the market in 1846. Most of the slaves went with her to live in Clarke County, where she moved in with her son, Lorenzo. Weeds and disrepair dimmed the beauty of her former home. The newspaper advertisement for its sale was run in the *Alexandria Gazette,* and it naturally mentioned that the estate was "once a part of Mount Vernon." Two thousand thirty acres were on the market, with barns, stables, a corn house, sheds, and a large stone mill. "The dwelling house is not surpassed by any in Virginia in construction, style of finish, and situation, being on a high hill in a grove of fine oaks, commanding a beautiful view of the river in front. . . . " And a little bait was cast toward Washington, D.C., where a rich person or an exiled prince might bite: "This place offers to those fond of field sports and good living peculiar advantages."

The property was sold to a company of Quakers from New Jersey and Pennsylvania in the name of their leader, Jacob Troth. To meet the price, they began cutting trees, not only in the nearly one thousand acres of woodland, but also in the park around the house. Nelly returned and wrote to a friend: "[Y]ou would not recognize it *now*—I went to see it when last in Alex[andria]—all the trees, the hedge, the flower knot, my precious Agnes's

Grove, the tall pine Washington, *all gone*. . . ." Thus one more affront to a life that had once seemed golden. But Troth's Quakers made Woodlawn revive financially, if modestly, when other Virginia farms were going under. The subdivision of the estate into smaller farms began within a decade.

After John Rogers Cooper married Encarnacion Vallejo, the couple built their Monterey home, known today as the Cooper-Molera Adobe (both, Elkinton Collection, Monterey State Historic Park)

In the viewpoint of many Americans, and not the least many Virginians, the answer to financial woes was to go to new land. The western territory was the utter fascination of the age. Angela Conrad wrote dreamily to her husband in 1837, "I have often wished to see what was passing beyond the mountains." Newspapers were filled with accounts of the revolution in Texas and adventures on the Santa Fe Trail, as well as reports by sea captains and sailors from the Pacific Coast. American discontent with the Mexican presence in those regions showed in a wave of anti-Catholicism. The otherwise kindly Mary Clara Weeks's vituperative attitude against Catholics probably came from this general feeling as much as her prejudice against her French neighbors. From the Shadows the trip overland to the eastern part of Mexican Texas had been only about two days in good weather. After Texas independence in 1836, the western border of the Republic of Texas lay only God knew where, perhaps a thousand miles into the desert. Today El Paso, at the western tip of Texas, is closer to San Diego, California, than it is to the Bayou Teche country. Most of the land between there and the Pacific Ocean was considered useless until some years later when the railroads made it accessible. In the 1830s and 1840s people paid it little attention, but some Americans took an interest in Mexican California.

California, reached by sea, seemed more like Mexico than any place else, and the best of the towns along the California coast at this time was Monterey. Visiting there in 1834, Richard Henry Dana found it a whitewashed village of one-story houses "built of *adobes*, that is, clay made into large bricks, about a foot and a half square, and three or four inches thick, and hardened in the sun. . . . The floors are generally of earth, the windows grated without glass; and the doors, which are seldom shut, open directly into the common room, there being no entries. Some of the more wealthy inhabitants have glass to their windows, and board floors." Following the Spanish tradition, there were no fireplaces until the 1830s. The cooking was done outside under the sky or in detached cookhouses. For warmth inside, charcoal braziers or vented fires sometimes were used. For furniture there were a few heavy-cut wooden beds, stools, tables, locally made, and trunks or chests that contained the valuable textiles, and sometimes a little plate, by which the Spanish in the New World always measured wealth and moved around wherever they went.

This inventory imparts the flavor of John Rogers Cooper's house built in Monterey about 1832. Cooper, a New Englander of British birth, had long been at sea before settling down in Monterey in 1827. As a young man of twenty-eight he signed as second mate aboard the *Thaddeus* in Boston,

The Coopers' home was begun in the 1830s, a rather typical Mexican-style house built of sun-dried adobe blocks. The second story was added some years later in a modernizing along Anglo-American lines (David Livingston)

which bore the first missionaries to Hawaii in 1819. Ports of call in Honolulu, Canton, and along the South American coast were familiar to him, and he had rounded Cape Horn and the Cape of Good Hope probably more times than he could remember. As a boarder in the adobe residence of the somewhat profligate Ignacio Vallejo, a sergeant at the presidio who was well known in Monterey, he fell in love with the daughter Encarnacion. On April 14, 1827, he complied with Mexican law and became a Catholic, so he and Encarnacion could be married, which took place four months later. The groom was thirty-six and the bride half that age. Of the event the toughened seaman wrote, toward the close of a long and active career, "I put it down as the one thing done right in my life." A few years after his marriage he loosened his legal restraints by becoming a citizen of Mexico.

This was a happy couple, well established by 1832 in the thick-walled, one-and-a-half-story house of adobe. Cooper opened a store in which he stocked goods from the United States, the South Pacific, and China. Although always distinctly an *Inglés,* for the language he spoke the most easily was English, he was attached through Encarnacion to the Vallejos. For an outsider to set himself up well in the region, a Mexican marriage was a good idea. Cooper had made such an alliance. Encarnacion's brother Mariano Vallejo glorified the name in years to come, but for the time the Vallejos provided entrée to the establishment, if only for being Mexican.

The decades of the 1820s and 1830s were marked by opportunity for those in the outer domains of a Mexico independent from Spain since 1821. For the government the years were stormy, with repeated turnovers of

Above: This large room in the Cooper-Molera Adobe, with its board floors and plastered adobe walls, has been restored to reflect its appearance in 1845. Right: In the large patio, the ground was swept with brooms, and vegetables and herbs such as these were planted in beds, rather than rows. The low, sloping roof of tiles marks the old residence, while subsidiary buildings, both original and from later years, flank the patio's outer perimeter (both, David Livingston)

political rule. All manner of experiments took place. There was even the brief ill-starred reign of the emperor Augustín Iturbide. His widow fled in exile to Washington, where she wept on the shoulder of Susan Decatur, widow of another man who had died before gunfire, although of a sort considered by some more honorable than Iturbide's firing squad. For Mexico, a constant theme of democracy led to many laws intended to overpower the surviving institutions of the Spanish crown, notably the church, with its vast lands.

This political movement washed ashore in California in the 1820s. There the organizational structure, as in northern Mexico in colonial times, consisted of *presidios* or forts extending from San Francisco in the north to San Diego in the south, protecting ports, as well as mission estates established in the eighteenth century to convert and educate the Indians in Latin ways. When Mexican lawmakers ordered the disposition of mission lands to Mexican citizens, entrepreneurs swarmed to California. For the most part, those already there got the first rewards and turned the old mission domains into *ranchos*. The Indians, freed now from the padres, were reduced by the *rancheros* to a status little better than slavery, perhaps worse.

Juan Bautista Rogers Cooper, as John Cooper, citizen of Mexico, was officially known in legal documents, acquired large tracts of land. His great ranches in Marin County, on the Salinas River, and in the Big Sur made his heirs richer than he would ever be. Until about 1850 Cooper himself was nearly always short of money, yet, unlike David Weeks, he did not succumb to melancholy; he built high hopes on the promise of wealth yet to be made.

Many like Cooper migrated to California. Each one saw the immediate advantage of a good marriage into a Mexican family, even the Mexicans themselves, who came with letters of introduction and favorable government appointments. In Monterey single women had many swains. Such a lover presented himself to Encarnacion Cooper's sister Prudenciana. He was a grand gentleman from Spain named Don José Galo Amesti, and he was on the make for riches.

He arrived in 1822, during the reign of Iturbide, with bright promises, and Prudenciana became his bride soon after. Don José acquired a large parcel of land, probably by government grant; then came the downfall of the Iturbide government, and he and Prudenciana went at once to the seclusion of their rancho near Santa Cruz, where they lived quietly for a decade. In 1832 they returned to Monterey so he could assume public office. Just how much the office of first *alcalde mayor*, or mayor, of Monterey had cost Don José Amesti is not known. It is not recorded whether he stood for election or went in person to Mexico City to politick for the post. Suffice it to say, he had the job—a good one in which to increase one's inventory.

Two years after his return to town, the *alcalde mayor* built his house, across the street from his in-laws, the Coopers. It was a four-room Mexican-style house of adobe, one story, probably not unlike the Cooper house, and is

the early part of the house we know today as Casa Amesti. The thick walls appear to have been whitewashed. Typically, domestic cloth was stretched over the ceilings and sometimes also whitewashed, to keep the dirt from sifting through. The house may have had wooden floors, although the earth moistened with oxblood and packed hard made a fine surface as durable as the low-fired flooring tiles one saw in Mexico. Amesti's house, unlike Cooper's, now bears no resemblance to what it was, for it is completely incorporated into a larger house.

We know little about the lives lived in the houses of the two sisters. Spanish was spoken at home, of course, and Cooper necessarily learned it to survive in California. He was better educated than his in-laws, but he was a foreigner, and his domestic life seems to have been Mexican, even though the setting may have had an Anglo-American flavor, with some furnishings one associates with New England at the time. Encarnacion Cooper was a handsome, capable woman who managed a house crowded with company and did church work in the community. She liked to visit her brother Mariano at his ranch to the north. Her sister Prudenciana returned from the ranch to Monterey severely handicapped by a spinal disorder suffered during the birth of her first child, Carmen. In contrast to the happy Coopers, Casa Amesti is remembered as being pressed under the thumb of the overbearing Don José, who was seventeen years older than Prudenciana and never hesitated to remind her that he was in charge.

Like the plantation masters in the world of the Weekses and the Draytons, the great *rancheros* were lords of all that was around them from animals to people, not least the oppressed Indian workers, and all but the most clever of wives were subject to this domination. Doña Prudenciana, a gentlewoman like all of the Vallejo women, was wholly lacking in the defiant spirit of some of them. Encarnacion had six children; Prudenciana had three, but she adopted more, little ones left without parents. Refusing to brood in seclusion over her lot, she absorbed herself in her church work and hobbled with her Indian maids to the mission to serve where she could in helping the poor. Monterey remembered her long after it had forgotten Don José.

It is not difficult to imagine these *Californios*, although surviving pictures show them only in old age. The sisters kept house with Indian servants in their adobes and wore the fancy clothing of their class, the cloth-of-gold, the *mantillas* of China silk, which hung over loose, full skirts that fell to the ankles. Their blouses were gathered full, showing some bosom, as well as lockets and crosses. Like practically all Mexican women they must have smoked constantly, puffing the flat, hand-rolled cigars that were a staple in any home. Their husbands surely smoked too and dressed in what was almost a uniform throughout Latin America. A *gente de razón* had finer materials in his clothing than a man of lesser rank, but generally the form of the clothes was the same, from the stiff, broad-brimmed, low-crowned black hat, to the short, fancy-braided jacket extending only to the black or red-sashed waist, to the long-tailed shirt, folded between the legs, to the tight, velveteen breeches, split to the knees, for horsemen's convenience, revealing silk hose and slippers or high boots. The finish was the broadcloth *pancho;* plain or fancy, this togalike drapery made its statement about the personality of the man. Yankee John Cooper never affected this dress, but wore white trousers and a blue coat. Be certain that it was the regular costume of Don José Amesti.

Men of substance were often away on business among the *ranchos* and four presidio towns on the coast. Cooper went to sea for the Mexican government and never again had a vessel of his own. Don José traveled by land, in company with Indian attendants. Mexican society expected a gentleman to be a good horseman — alas for the horse. The *Californios,* in the tradition of Spain, rode furiously over the open land, demanding full exertion from their mounts, with encouragement from spiked bits and cruel spurs that made blood run down the hind legs of the beasts and glisten in the sun. For Amesti to ride to San Francisco was to load his heavy, broad-pommeled Spanish saddle on his horse and literally race along the route, following the ocean at points. The region was full of horses running loose. When one horse was spent, Don José or his attendant lassoed another in a pasture and likewise rode it down, until time to obtain another. Three or four horses were required for the trip from Monterey to San Francisco.

John Cooper was a good moneymaker but took big risks. He was, however, poor at keeping his accounts and needed an office manager, a clerk he could trust. It seemed to him a good idea to find a relative back in New England, so he wrote asking for candidates. Cooper's younger half-brother, the headstrong Thomas Larkin, who had declared himself grown, while still in his teens, had gone down to North Carolina to seek his fortune — which did not materialize. A relative passed on to him Cooper's letter. He hesitated, hoping a better opportunity might appear, but at last he headed west. Larkin was received in Monterey with some eagerness as the one who was expected to put Cooper's books in order and help him evade financial ruin.

When he finally arrived, after an unexpected stopover in Hawaii, he went to the Coopers along with a fellow passenger, Rachel Holmes; she was the wife of a Danish sea captain and a friend of Cooper's. There she awaited her husband. It was not long before she and Larkin became lovers, if the fire had not ignited already aboard ship. Encarnacion, with the pragmatism in such matters sometimes found among the Mexican gentry, looked the other way. By late spring 1832 Rachel was pregnant. So when the news came in the summer that her husband had died of a fever, her grief was not without bounds. Baby Isabel Ana was baptized the following winter but lived

Top: Casa Amesti has had a renowned garden for most of its years. The one visible today was planted in the early 1920s (David Livingston). Above: An old view from about 1910, by R. J. Arnold, records the garden of Casa Amesti as the Amesti descendants had it in later years (Pat Hathaway Collection). Left: The original garden wall and gate, seen about 1920, evoke the romance that made old adobes so popular (Pat Hathaway Collection)

only a few months. Larkin pondered the situation, hesitating to do the right thing. At last something made him propose, perhaps the healthy inheritance left Rachel by the Dane. After a year they took a ship out from Santa Barbara into the Pacific sunset and were married by John Coffin Jones, an entrepreneur who was the self-styled "U.S. consul" to Hawaii.

Cooper's financial problems were settled eventually by selling land to raise cash, a thing he, as a speculator, disliked, for he was one who tended to cling fast to what he had acquired. Grudgingly he pared himself of some of his real estate, in a successful effort to save most of his *ranchos*. To satisfy some debts in October 1833 he gave up half of his Monterey house to John Coffin Jones. The severed half changed hands several times after that, but Cooper never bought it back. On occasion he considered returning to New England, but the idea never went far with his wife. Encarnacion was one pillar in the support of her family, and her brother Mariano was the other. Neither of them was likely to be drawn away for long. She moved her widowed mother into the Casa Cooper, along with her mother's servants and several of the younger relatives dependent on the mother. From time to time Vallejos filled the house to capacity and more. Rather than sell more land than he had to, Cooper remained a sea captain for long periods to keep a flow of cash into his purse. Holding onto land and paying debts while maintaining nearly full-time work as a sea captain made for a busy life. In spite of the aggravations this entailed, his labors and his land would one day make him a rich man.

Larkin was soon on his own, ambitious and at times ruthless. Disputes with his half-brother may have helped him make the decision to branch out, but they remained friends, only with different ideas about how things should be done. Larkin saw opportunity all around him, just as Cooper always had, and he needed time and freedom. He and Rachel moved to the country, to Cooper's property, where a son was born. Allowing himself plenty of room to get about and become known among the *Californios*, Larkin quickly entered the business world on practically every level. He dealt in land and invested in shipping and quickly prospered; he would turn over any land or merchandise to make a profit. On the other hand, "My brother," he wrote of Cooper, "has $100,000 of land but will not sell."

In 1835 Larkin started the long process of building his house, which remains one of the fine sights of old Monterey. It was made of adobe, but was otherwise wholly American rather than Mexican in character. Rising a full two stories, the house dominated its corner lot. It was surrounded on two sides by double-deck porches, all eventually under a hipped roof, giving it the flavor of the Gulf Coast or the Caribbean, not so much of California. The rooms opened off a long central hallway running front to back and containing a long, Yankee-looking staircase. There were glass windows. And the most foreign feature of all, it had fireplaces.

Here, in the 1840s, Larkin began his undercover activities as American consul in Monterey, making secret reports to the U.S. Department of State on personalities and activities in California. His circle expanded usefully to include associations and acquaintances all along the California coast, and his letters to Washington were read by the president. Larkin's house was known as a place of delightful hospitality to anyone visiting the city from the South Pacific, Mexico, South America, Hawaii, or the United States. Few guests probably realized that they and their business, described in conversations fueled by wine, made text for Larkin's regular reports.

The Amestis, the Coopers, and the Larkins formed a visible family group in Monterey. As the 1840s wore on, the issue of California's future as an American state became embroiled in a melodrama of military encounters and other conflicts, usually involving in one way or another Mariano Vallejo, brother of Encarnacion and Prudenciana. Vallejo was imprisoned during the famous Bear Flag Revolt of 1846, but he was soon set free to return to his plotting in favor of the Americans. By the time the war between the United States and Mexico actually started in 1846, American ships already were anchored in the harbor of Monterey.

Through the doors of the homes of the Monterey circle passed the luminaries of the Mexican War in California: Captain John Drake Sloat, Commodore Robert Stockton, General Stephen Watts Kearney, John Charles Fremont and his wife, Jessie Benton Fremont, Kit Carson, William Tecumseh Sherman—and youthful and adventurous Lieutenant Edward Fitzgerald Beale, who remained a Californian but one day owned Decatur House in Washington. Stars and stripes flew over Monterey early in the war, and by its close in 1848 *gringos* were everywhere. Most of the newcomers considered it the best town in California. Monterey might have been the Golden State's great metropolis but for the discovery of gold to the north, near Sacramento, some months before the end of the war. The gold rush was felt in Monterey in the loss of its most prominent citizens to business opportunity northward, closer to the gold diggings. By the 1860s Don José Amesti, John Cooper, and Thomas Larkin and their families all ended up in San Francisco, after departing with little notice, never to live in Monterey again.

Larkin sold his house. Amesti gave his to his daughter Carmen, who was newly married to a mysterious, lupine Scot named James McKinley, with whom she lived a stormy, unhappy life; they later divorced. John Cooper, of course, kept his house. During the 1850s the Amesti and Cooper houses were Americanized to keep up with passing time, somewhat in the Larkin House manner; upper stories were added to each, along with varied Yankee amenities such as a central hallway, glass windows, and fireplaces. Fashionable mahogany furniture was acquired, along with fancy painted china. The two houses were cherished for generations by descendants of their builders. In the case of the Coopers' house, the errant half traded for a debt in 1833 was regained in 1900, uniting the property once more. Juan Bautista Rogers Cooper would have been pleased.

Houses Divided

O nly a short walk from the driveway at Drayton Hall is a cemetery that tradition holds was established by the Draytons in colonial times for their slaves. It is the only cemetery at Drayton Hall, and a recent cutting away of weeds and brambles indicates that it is larger than anyone had thought. The scattered gravestones are relatively new. Most of the graves are unmarked. Late afternoon light rakes across the cleared ground in such a way as to emphasize numerous slight sinks in the sandy earth that identify row after row of very old graves. The shadow cenotaphs of forgotten people make this spot seem all the more lonely.

African-born slaves and English-born indentured servants alike had worked the fields of early American plantations. After the Revolution the tenuous indentured servants of many hues went away, leaving black slaves as the work force. Slavery fared even in the Age of Reason and the Enlightenment, through the Declaration of Independence and the ratification of the Constitution—and seventy years later, in the 1850s, one could stand in the same graveyard at Drayton Hall and contemplate a plantation enterprise that had been run with slave labor for well over a hundred years. Already it was hard for an outsider to the southern culture to imagine without repulsion.

By the 1850s the institution of slavery was under attack. Debates between those pro and con haunted every political event and every politician's most troubled dreaming. Expansion of slave holding into the new regions of the West had dramatically increased antislavery feeling in the North and old Northwest. The nation was consumed with the expansion of slavery beyond its southern confines. Anger was universal, and violence erupted on many levels, a little among the slaves themselves, but much with the lawmakers. The battles became protracted. During Jackson's presidency, in the heyday of South Carolina's Senator John C. Calhoun, the Palmetto State was the testing ground for state's rights defiance of federal authority, by declaring null and void by state convention any locally objectionable acts of Congress. While Jackson had prevailed, the state found a new identity as the defender of southern interests. Premonitions were felt at Drayton Hall, whose master, Charles Drayton II, wrote to his son in 1833 that the emotion-charged emancipation movement, "as started in England, if realized, will transfer a great bearing on the United States: of course the whole evil will fall on the Southern section—Already does[. G]reat though secret—anxiety cloud our atmosphere! Therefore planters must entertain views of the future different from those of existing times."

Neither he nor the son lived to see the fires really flare. When that finally came about, in the 1850s, the master of Drayton Hall was a boy only in his teens, the son of the third Charles, who had died young. Charles Henry Drayton seems to have been the legal ruler of his Ashley River kingdom from the age of five. As a strong boy of fourteen in 1860, he had developed a planter's bearing, as well as a mind of his own. He lived with his widowed mother, Sarah, sometimes at Drayton Hall but mostly in a Charleston house, for he attended school in the city. The family had already started a pattern of using Drayton Hall more in the mild months, and by this time they were joining other South Carolina Low Country folk at fever-free summer retreats in the mountains of North Carolina. It may be that Drayton Hall retained only a few of its furnishings by the 1850s.

Charles loved the plantation and its endless freedoms. He and some of his numerous cousins romped the fields and woods. In addition to the twenty-five adult slaves were nineteen children, enough of them boys Charles's age so that he probably never lacked playmates for horseback rides and games or comrades with whom he might hunt birds along the abandoned, mirror-like rice fields or fish in the Ashley. Drayton Hall had been turned from rice to cotton, an attempt—and perhaps no more than that—to take advantage of the large market in the 1850s for long staple cotton. It was not the plantation it had once been. Charles's Uncle John, a doctor in a long line of Drayton doctors, was administrator of his property; he was an amiable, wry man of twenty-eight in 1860 and an attentive friend to the fatherless boy. Of the mother, Sarah, we know little, except that she did not have much hold on Charles, who had a touch of old John Drayton's shrewdness and negotiated hard when necessary to have his own way. Nephew and uncle enjoyed an easy relationship then and for the rest of their lives. The physician watched closely to assure the well-being of the boy.

Events linked to the coming explosion of the Civil War must have seemed at once distant and crazily close to the Draytons. Charleston itself was a festering sore of threatened hostilities. Already in the 1850s the lifeblood of the city pumped with false youth. The old town, its business house by no means in order, beat its war drums before the world, presuming to represent all of the South, when in fact most of the southern states were not in such a hurry. John Drayton was a nominal supporter of state's rights, with conditions, although cousins of his had moved to the Northeast because they could not bear the insularity of Charleston. Considerations that made older men pause, however, did not hinder master Charles. He was thrilled by the drumbeats and was ready for war.

The drama of the approaching cataclysm was played in many places before it all came together to be seen as one event. Washington was the principal scene; here the future was foreshadowed in the interactions of people from all of the regions. As always, Stephen and Susan Decatur's tall brick house looked down on the parade of history, sometimes sheltering episodes and famous people. In the last years of the 1850s it was often vacant, at times rented out. Susan Decatur had long since sold it. From the window that Martin Van Buren had cut in the south wall, one could still see the White House as clearly as from a crow's nest above the sea of trees; the president's windows and glass conservatory roof were now aglow nightly with the gaslight that shone down on his splendid entertainments, veneers created by James Buchanan to hide the terrible tensions in the political city. Buchanan's White House would be remembered as the nearest the place was ever allowed to seem like a royal court. If the effort had proved politically fatal to a few of his predecessors, now it seemed harmless. Lines of carriages ringed Lafayette Park, awaiting their turn to enter the iron gates, southerners and Yankees in attendance but not comfortable together.

While Decatur House still occupied a prominent place in the best neighborhood in town, it had only one golden moment in this antebellum period. A shuttered existence was interrupted when the famous Louisiana senator Judah Philips Benjamin was briefly a rent-paying tenant. Considered the most brilliant maritime lawyer of his day, the native South Carolinian entered politics from his adopted state and followed its state's rights passions, but as a wise moderate. A poor boy from the docks of Charleston who had made good in New Orleans, Benjamin spent money on Decatur House, although the extent of his work is not known. To its old-fashioned rooms he moved the gilded chairs and sofas, the inlaid tabourets, the mirrors and statues that had adorned the galleried mansion at his sugar plantation, Bellechasse, below New Orleans. Why so much attention to a rented

Judah P. Benjamin, senator from Louisiana, was photographed by Mathew Brady at about the time he lived in Decatur House, hoping its magic would win back his wife (Library of Congress)

house? Was this yet another politician making a splash in Washington? Politics it was indeed, but not the usual sort; this was domestic, and it might better have been called marital diplomacy. Senator Benjamin hoped to attract his estranged wife, Natalie, from a self-imposed exile in Paris. They had been separated off and on for fifteen years.

It seemed a good plan, considering that the temperamental Natalie, a high-born Creole from New Orleans, had an appetite for magnificence and gaiety. The whole world was watching Washington. Benjamin's personality had never required a setting; hers, not so gregarious, apparently did, and Decatur House was perfect. She did return, bringing with her Ninette, their teenage daughter. Ninette entered convent school in Georgetown, to which an elegant coach transported her every day. Political society came to call. After they left, they remembered more about the house than about Natalie. Those who did take note of her found her either withdrawn or silly, and a few detected just a touch of antisemitism, not so curious for a Catholic but surprising for one married to a Jew. There were grand dinners to delight her, and many evenings at the White House. She seemed pleased.

After a short while, however, she packed up and she and Ninette returned to France. Embarrassed and angry, Benjamin rambled about his house alone. At last he decided not to try again. He summoned an auctioneer, and on the spot the treasures of Bellechasse fell under the hammer. "Everyone in Washington now thronged to see the beautiful things," recalled a senator's wife who had called on Natalie, "and many purchased specimens from among them. . . ." Not two decades later, when it seemed that a hundred years had passed by—and the Civil War was long over—the former senator and Confederate cabinet member, by then in his ninth life as a distinguished London lawyer, joined Natalie in Paris, and the two old people were reunited once and for all. At Decatur House no mark commemorates their stay in architecture, unless it is the brightly painted checkerboard patterns on the floors that still lie buried beneath subsequent surfaces, upstairs and down, and may be part of the decorations that were to bring Natalie home again.

When Benjamin closed and locked Decatur House in 1860, the last occupant before the Civil War, he did so unnoticed. Politics by then claimed all of the attention. Event after event, culminating in the fall with Lincoln's election, drew the nation closer to civil war, as sectional identities became ever sharper, against a background of anxious waiting. No place seemed too remote and peaceful to be trespassed on by the anger and disruption if not of politics, certainly of the general bad temper of the times. An example of one who experienced those times on several levels was James Murray Mason, firebrand and state's-rights member of the U.S. Senate from Virginia, colleague of Judah Benjamin and announced political successor to John C. Calhoun.

Grandson of George Mason, author of the Virginia Bill of Rights—copied by practically every democratic nation since—James Mason in his orations often invoked the Spirit of '76, which he believed he was more than entitled to do by blood. The Founders were in their graves, and many such interpreters came to the fore by the 1850s. With his fellow legislators, Mason dined at Buchanan's White House. A social sort of fellow, he was along when the Prince of Wales (later King Edward VII) made a state visit in 1860 and placed a wreath on the tomb of Washington. When Mason was not in Washington, he was at home with his large family in Winchester, Virginia, or in Germantown, Pennsylvania, at his wife's ancestral home, Cliveden.

James Mason and Eliza Chew met in the bosom of her family, he a southern youth in school at the University of Pennsylvania who was often entertained by the Chews. When Mason established himself as a lawyer in Winchester, he and Eliza were married and returned to the Shenandoah Valley to join the Hites of Belle Grove and other gentry in an abundant but unadorned life. One of their children remembered their house, Selma, as a "substantial and comfortable stone dwelling, beautifully located upon such high ground that it commanded a fine view of the surrounding country, and it looked down upon the town, which made a very pretty picture, as it seemed to nestle at the foot of the Blue Ridge Mountains."

In 1860 James and Eliza Mason celebrated thirty-eight years of marriage. It was a happy partnership, but one that in the last decade gained its share of burdens. Benjamin Chew, Jr., son of the colonial chief justice, had been a best friend and mentor to James Mason. Chew was an odd and by nature extremely conservative man who wore eighteenth-century-style small clothes and quaint old silver shoe buckles and tied his long hair in a queue until the day he died. His fatherly relationship with Mason was unusually close for in-laws. Each sensed a broader kinship in being from old and distinguished families. That both had southern connections, too, was not overlooked.

Chew's death in 1844 distressed Mason deeply. He replaced this idol with his political ideal, John C. Calhoun, and followed the old warhorse in his last years as a sort of apostle. They shared living quarters in Washington. Calhoun selected Mason to read his speech at the debates over the Compromise of 1850, while the Nullifier sat nearby silent and dying, slumped in his chair, surveying the chamber with that fierce glare of his. Calhoun died a short time after, leaving the forum to Mason, Jefferson Davis, and the others who would, within a decade, form the Confederate States of America. Mason was a member of the special party that accompanied Calhoun's remains by sea to a black-draped grieving Charleston. On his own, Mason helped further the cause of state's rights throughout the 1850s. He was set firmly in his southern views, yet even as author of the Fugitive Slave Act he was considered among the more conciliatory of the radicals in Congress. He was often in the news, praised down South, condemned up North.

As coexecutor of his father-in-law's estate with his brother-in-law Henry Banning Chew of Baltimore, Mason became embroiled also in a family con-

James Murray Mason, senator from Virginia and brother-in-law of Anne Sophia Penn Chew, was a fire-eating southern secessionist who loved the cool groves of Cliveden (Library of Congress)

troversy that held the will of Benjamin Chew, Jr., in limbo for two full decades. His Philadelphia brother-in-law, Colonel Benjamin Chew III, brought suit against the estate, halting the process of settlement and bringing on the prolonged legal battle. In apparent fear for the well-being of the old family home, Eliza Mason's unmarried sister, Anne Sophia Penn Chew, moved from her mother's residence in Philadelphia to Cliveden, where she established herself full time, very much under the legal advice and protection of James Mason and Henry Chew. That some sort of conflict had erupted between mother and daughter seems evident, because Colonel Ben was able to convince the widow Chew that the three other children, including Anne Sophia, were conspiring against her, and he persuaded his mother to join in the suit against them.

So it was a classic family war, with Cliveden's Anne Sophia the one with the most to lose. Colonel Ben and his mother removed many furnishings from Cliveden to his own home, leaving Anne Sophia in the house with what was left. Not long after, the sheriff served this sad granddaughter of the mighty colonial justice with an eviction notice. She called to her southern kin for help. James Mason, responding to his wife's tears over her terrified sister, saved the day. He was not only a smart lawyer, but also a mean one, and he turned his skills against Colonel Ben. Henry Chew gave his approval but managed to steer clear of most of the action. Among the issues fought over was management of the Maryland plantations and slaves. The wealth the Chews had known for so long from that source had shrunk, and it was easier to blame one another than external forces such as the national panic that bore hard on all of the Chews.

In 1857, the year of the panic, a hero appeared in Anne Sophia Chew's life in the form of her nephew Samuel, amiable and good-hearted son of Henry Chew. Sam Chew could have stepped whole from the pages of one of Hawthorne's novels, a good man to save the day. He moved from Baltimore to Philadelphia to practice law with his Philadelphia relatives, and he unpacked his bag at Cliveden. His sunny presence began to light the dark rooms. Anne Sophia, the thin, sharp-featured woman who stood as straight as a warrior, may have been helpless in a sense but she was also a survivor, and she determined to keep this youthful champion close by. Within a year Sam was happily commuting from Cliveden into the city. Bright and sensitive, he was a good listener who soon took a fancy to Cliveden's past. Anne Sophia spun her web, telling him how the British had held out within its thick walls, and how Major André had flattered Aunt Peggy Chew, who accepted pretty pictures drawn by him. From a drawer Anne Sophia produced André's sketches for her nephew to study in utter wonder.

Sam, put to the task of finding a way to save his aunt's home, became convinced that she must own Cliveden outright. He effected a division with the other relatives and began buying their shares. Some property was subdivided. He included money of his own, and at last the title came to him and Anne Sophia. Ending up with more money than had been expected, Anne Sophia later siphoned off some of it to enclose the curving breezeway between the house and kitchen, modernize the kitchen, and install a partial heating system. But in 1860 all of these improvements were not in place. "We got in at Cliveden and had some talk with Miss Chew . . . ," wrote a visitor. "[T]he house and grounds [are] woefully out of repair." Yet a whole new sequence in the story of the old house had begun.

Elsewhere, through the months of 1860, the American people tried to contemplate the nation about to blow up. People, it seemed, had lost their minds. Lincoln's nomination and the ensuing campaign stirred emotions everywhere. Down south in Louisiana, the streets of New Orleans were noisy with political rallies calling for Louisiana's secession from the Union. Mary Clara Weeks Moore of the Shadows, an old woman now, had once loved to go to the city. She would now have threaded through crowded streets and found the endless political festival frightening in a way that would make her glad to return to the quiet of the Shadows. She had asked her husband to procure for her a copy of *Uncle Tom's Cabin* years before, when it was new. What must have been her thoughts on that melodrama, filled with helpless blacks and evil Yankees, that dead-on-the-mark attack on slavery at its own most sacred and sentimental defenses?

David Weeks, who worried so over money, had always admonished her to save and not to spend. Now the complaint was current in the Weeks family finances; as her son put it, "We have been dancing too fast to the music." To recover some money, she, like the Chews at Cliveden, began subdividing her property at the Shadows. Surveyors drove stakes; trees were felled; a house began to rise in view of her upper gallery. It was not bad to have close neighbors when one got old. Mary Clara planted her corn and peas, tended her roses, and kept her home nicely. She had always accepted the need to change, and now she herself had changed with age. Among her papers is an order for false teeth. And she asked that bells be installed in the house to summon the servants, because she was too infirm to "get up all the time" and call them from the gallery.

Lincoln was elected president in November 1860, and in December South Carolina seceded from the Union. Other states followed in the early months of 1861. In April the war began in earnest, with the firing on Fort Sumter in Charleston Harbor. James Mason and Judah Benjamin already had resigned from Congress and hurried from Washington by train to Alabama to help with the formation of the new Confederate government. After the guns sounded over Fort Sumter, the fourteen-year-old master of Drayton Hall, Charles Henry Drayton, awaited his opportunity to go to war. Kept at home with threats, he soon ran away to serve in the army as a courier. Neither letters nor tears brought Sarah Drayton success in her four-year campaign to bring her boy home to Charleston.

Seven of the ten houses described so far were in the South and near the scenes of military action. Confederate troops camped at Montpelier at different times; courts-martial were held in the house. The neighborhood of Woodlawn, so close to Washington, was occupied by federal forces immediately after the war began. Nelly Lewis's big red brick house was owned by John Mason and his wife, Rachel, who was a cousin of Abraham Lincoln. They occupied the house and used it occasionally for meetings of the Woodlawn Baptist Church, which they founded there. The house held to its Washington memories, although with a cast of mildew and neglect. A new house made of wood, smaller and warmer and drier, stood a distance away, still in view of the old house and the panorama of the Potomac River beyond Mount Vernon. It became the main residence at Woodlawn.

Oatlands was at times painfully close to the battlegrounds. The widowed Elizabeth Carter packed up and moved most of her belongings to a place she considered safer, leaving a few pieces of furniture and pictures. Troops billeted in the house for a short time. Sons Benjamin and George Carter served in the Confederate army, and when they were near home they liked to camp out in the sparse rooms where they had grown up. On October 13, 1863, George married Kate W. Powell at Trinity Episcopal Church in Upperville. By Christmas they were living at Oatlands with his mother.

Louisiana fell to Union forces early in the war. Family letters at the Shadows describe the looting of houses, the tearing up of carpets, the taking away of horses and cows. The aged Mary Clara Weeks Moore followed all of the war news with interest, keeping her own house wholly intact. John Moore had been a member of the Louisiana secession convention and signed the document that declared his state seceded from the Union. Away serving in the Confederate legislature, he offered no protection for his wife at home. Union steamers at last arrived on Bayou Teche. General Nathaniel P. Banks, fresh from unsuccessful command in the valley of Virginia,

John and Rachel Mason (at far right) posed in front of Woodlawn with fellow members of the Woodlawn Baptist Church, which used the house for services until a permanent building was erected (Woodlawn)

ordered the ground-floor rooms of the Shadows set aside as offices for the provost marshal. Mary Clara was left comfortably situated in her usual living quarters upstairs, but her children, fearing the soldiers' presence, finally convinced her to leave. After packing to depart the next day, she died in her sleep that night. Burial took place in the yard at the Shadows, apparently undisturbed by the visitors in blue. She lived to hear the news that her grandson David Weeks Magill, wounded near New Orleans in 1862, was killed at Vicksburg in the summer of 1863.

Far behind Union lines, in the relative freedom of the East, Cliveden looked timeless and unchanged. But nothing is timeless and nothing remains unchanged. Samuel Chew was happy with his decision to remain with his Aunt Anne Sophia, whom he had largely saved from the machinations of her brother. In 1861 he married Mary Johnson Brown, daughter of a wealthy Philadelphia merchant and manufacturer of printed cotton cloth. The aunt was not enthusiastic, and the bride herself studied the foreboding stone house with some dismay. But Sam and Mary were very much in love, and the problems between the two women, which were to continue for thirty years, failed in every instance to alter that. A caller at Cliveden wrote: "The whole thing struck me rather strangely, the imposing old house with its mutilated statues and grim stone lions, the slipshod Irish chambermaid who ushered us in, the fine large rooms almost destitute of furniture, in which a few heavy, shabby old articles contrasted strangely with one or two little modern knickknacks. . . . [I]t seemed such a strange old place for two young people to be beginning their lives in."

War's clamor seemed far away from Cliveden's grove, but it was not. Sam Chew was in the city every day, so he cannot have missed the draft riots and the parading soldiers. He was the age to go to war himself, but for some reason he was able to avoid it. The Chew name was dragged through the press in Philadelphia and New York at the outset of the war, to offend James Mason. Appointed to represent the Confederate government in Britain, Mason was rumored to have been arrested in Philadelphia for treason while en route to England. His and Eliza's Pennsylvania property was said to be confiscated. He was in fact arrested, but at sea aboard the *Trent*, and was taken to Boston to spend some months in prison, along with his colleague John Slidell and the secretary George Eustis (whose son appears at Oatlands in Virginia forty years later). A vindictive Colonel Benjamin Chew gave an interview in which he assured reporters that he would not raise a hand or interfere in any way to protect his relatives' property. The *New York Herald* reported that "several persons in and around Germantown—operators in town lots &c., and patriotically spirited gentlemen—are forwarding the matter."

Colonel Chew's malice toward his brother-in-law Mason was no more than his loathing for his brother Henry and his sister Anne Sophia. They may have considered themselves out of his reach, but through the press Chew vented his wrath at them all, even calling down the judgment of history in rattling an old skeleton that the illustrious Chews had been Tories during the American Revolution. This cut deep at Cliveden. Sam, now angry, proceeded with the lawsuits, vowing vengeance against his uncle. His father, embarrassed the most over the Tory accusations, wrote a defense in the matter that was to be read in the courtroom if the subject ever came up.

Life for the Chews at Cliveden was held together as best it could be. Their southern income was cut off. Tenants in the Baltimore rental properties refused to pay. The plantations in Maryland were fallow, and the slaves were gone. Anne Sophia, mortified by the ugly newspaper aspersions on her heritage, became ever more proud, defending the disrepair of Cliveden as "historic." Cliveden had but one mistress, and it was she. The unwelcome Mary, for all of her fine new money, was kept at a distance. Toward the close of the war Sam gave up his law practice and joined Mary's father, David Sands Brown, in his successful mercantile house and cotton cloth printing factory, where Brown was in need of a good lawyer he could trust. The cloth business was in transition while turning from the South as the source of cotton to other markets. Every step had to be made with extreme caution, and Sam proved wise and prudent at business. No known Chew heretofore had been in trade, but under this new status the Chews of Cliveden became rich again.

The Union's military strategies, revised by Ulysses S. Grant in the spring of 1864, were made with the upcoming presidential election in mind. Among the targets was Virginia's rich Shenandoah Valley. Federal forces had been a presence there in 1861 and 1862. Among their activities was to demolish James Murray Mason's house, plank by plank, stone by stone, until nothing whatsoever remained of it. Not for two years since then had much activity taken place in the valley. In Union eyes the region lay wide open, its apple orchards, wheat fields, herds, and flocks provisioning Robert E. Lee's formidable army. Winchester was the unvanquished gateway to Pennsylvania, Maryland, and the capital city. The daring Confederate Lieutenant General Jubal Early invaded Pennsylvania and made attacks on the outskirts of Washington before retreating to his haven in the valley. Embarrassment to Lincoln's administration for this audacity could be measured as political peril to the Republicans and an advantage to the Democrats.

In August General Grant ordered Major General Philip H. Sheridan to the valley with an army to stop Early. "It is desirable that nothing should be left to invite the enemy to return," added Grant. "Take all provisions, forage and stock . . . such as cannot be consumed, destroy. . . . [W]e want the Shenandoah Valley to remain a barren waste." Sheridan established his headquarters at Belle Grove, the old mansion of the long-dead Hites. It may

Two months before the Battle of Cedar Creek overtook Belle Grove, Major General Philip H. Sheridan was documented by James E. Taylor leaving the house on a reconnaisance mission (Western Reserve Historical Society)

have been vacant when Sheridan moved in. Owned since the year before the war by the Cooley brothers, Benjamin and John, who were farmers, it was farmed but was not likely the Cooley residence. The Hite furnishings had been sold. Old drawings made during the war show Belle Grove's rooms supplied only with military camp furniture.

The house became central to the Battle of Cedar Creek, October 19, 1864, which made Grant's dream of domination over the valley come true. Already, six days earlier, Jubal Early had fired on the house; the federals charged from Belle Grove across Cedar Creek in a short and bloody conflict that left two hundred Union soldiers and seventy-five Confederates dead. To Belle Grove the captured goods from the valley were brought to be taken away as military supplies. Cattle, corn, and barrels of flour and sugar were stockpiled with farm tools, guns, and ammunition. Forty-five enemy cannons were lined in soldierly rows, as were hundreds of vehicles of all kinds. Horses were rounded up by the hundred. More than a thousand prisoners loitered about playing cards and talking in the meadow beside the house.

By the foggy daybreak of October 19, military operations were in full tilt. Belle Grove then, as now, seemed to stand alone in the rolling, open landscape. On the long day of the battle the full panorama of the various military encounters spread out like a pageant to those who stood on the high points, looking on. The rail fences, with ragged clumps of trees, were damaged or gone, cut up for soldiers' firewood in the camps. Jubal Early, who had tormented his adversaries for a week, began with boldness and success. "In the struggle about the house . . . the blood of the contestants freely mingled and a host of dead strewed the ground," recorded a Union participant of the daybreak action around Belle Grove.

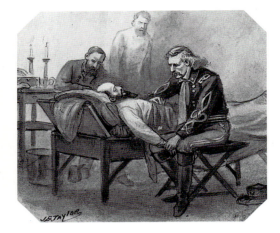

By mid-morning General Sheridan was on his way back to Belle Grove from Winchester. Hearing that the battle had started, he raced on horseback to his troops and raised Union morale to such a high point that the day turned to the federal forces. Sheridan sent his troops hard against Early's. After an hour Early began to weaken, and he eventually retreated. Dust settled. Wrote one witness: "When the fifteen hours of carnage had ceased, and the sun had gone down . . . there remained a scene more horrid than usual. The dead and dying of the two armies were commingled. Many of the wounded had dragged themselves to the streams in search of

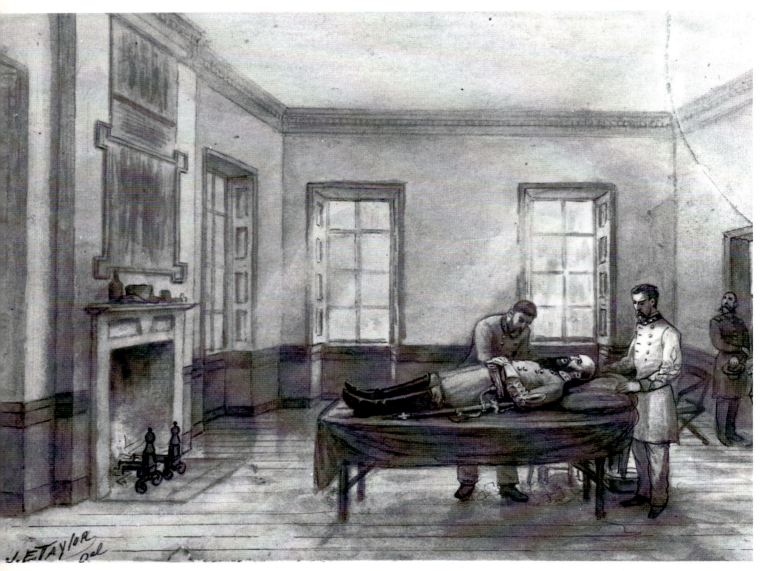

the first want of a wounded man—water. Many mangled and loose horses were straggling over the field. . . . Dead and dying men were found in the darkness almost everywhere. Cries of agony from the suffering victims were heard in all directions, and the moans of wounded animals added much to the horrors of the night." By dawn on October 20, Jubal Early was moving rapidly south from all of this, to his back the once-beautiful valley, war torn and lost to the Confederacy forever.

On the Atlantic coast, the city of Charleston finally gave up to the invaders from the north. It was February 18, 1865. Lincoln had been jubilantly reelected, crediting a significant part of his victory to the battle won in Belle Grove's fields. Charleston, like Moscow to Napoleon, was left to the victors. Most of the citizens had gone. Ruins were everywhere. Contrabands—as the ex-slaves who flocked to the federal armies were called—wandered the streets half-starved, looking to the victors to save them. The Yankees established martial law. Occupying officers begged in letters to their superiors that something be done about the sanitary conditions in the abandoned city, fearing an epidemic of yellow fever or smallpox by the advent of warm weather in March. By April, the month Lincoln was shot, the contrabands had been ordered out of Charleston, assigned to more healthful rural locations, to houses that were vacant.

At some point—it is not clear just when—the great houses along the Ashley River were put to the torch, one by one. Who set all of the fires is not known, although Union officers burned nearby Middleton. The reason Drayton Hall escaped is not documented indisputably. Legend says that it was saved by a resourceful man, and this cannot be wholly dismissed, for it was in the hands of such a person.

Dr. John Drayton had served the Confederate government on contract throughout the war, giving medical attention to black laborers at various South Carolina military sites. He went to his work on horseback and by boat, treating winter's pneumonia and summer's malaria and smallpox. This was a risky task not likely much in demand by doctors, and to his patients he can have seemed no less than a saint. At the war's end Drayton Hall is believed to have been occupied by blacks, perhaps some of those sent out of Charleston, and official records do show that the Freedmen's Bureau had established authority over the place. John Drayton was there, perhaps as a doctor for the contrabands; smallpox and cholera had made their feared appearance in Charleston and the Low Country, where chaos and death now reigned. Anticipating the fate that awaited his ancestral home, he put a notice on the house that victims of an epidemic were within—this warning was usually given by flagging windows or porches with sheets that could be seen from far away. Whoever burned the other Ashley River houses took heed and fled. The mansion survived, to greet Charles Henry Drayton, a toughened veteran of eighteen, when he came home from the war.

Opposite above: With the cheering and celebration of Union victory just outside Belle Grove's windows, General George Armstrong Custer stayed inside at the bedside of the mortally wounded Confederate General Stephen Dodson Ramseur. In the annals of the Valley Campaign, this would be remembered as "the midnight vigil." "What sublimer spectacle can be conceived," wrote James E. Taylor, who also sketched this scene of the former cadets at West Point who had been enemies on the battlefield. Opposite below: In the parlor at Belle Grove General Ramseur's body was embalmed by a Confederate surgeon, assisted by Ramseur's aide, Major Hutchinson. The general, wrote James E. Taylor, "with gauntleted hand over breast, emblematic of rest, and sword at side, presented a picture, even in death, of the ideal warrior" (both, Western Reserve Historical Society)

Victorian Ambitions

After four years of strife nothing in American life was left untouched, and the presence of change gave a marked character to the country. The broken South was a feature of the difference. But the South was relatively small compared to the larger part of the nation that had overwhelmed it, expelled its divisionist ideas, and, with a more spiritual and more complete sense of union than Americans had ever known before, pressed forward toward its perceived destiny that the United States become the greatest nation in the world.

The excitement of the present and the future did not mean that the past was entirely cast aside. Pasts of different kinds played intellectually on the people of the time. The most powerful was the immediate past—the one from which they were separated by war as though it were a gulf. Yet they remembered the years before, and this past of recollections came to mean much to them. They cast aside the romantic past represented in Lyndhurst's towers and Washington Irving's novels, which had thrilled them before the war. They turned now to images more real, true to actual experience: characters such as that 1840s boy Huckleberry Finn. In this way they could

Opposite: The grand staircase at Brucemore evokes baronial splendor within the tall-chimneyed Iowa mansion. Completed by Caroline Sinclair in 1886, Brucemore was named by its second owners, Irene and George Bruce Douglas, after the Scottish moors of Douglas's ancestral home. They remodeled the house in 1908, adding this butternut paneling and, in the 1920s, a mural of Wagner's Ring Cycle (Bradley Photographics)

Preceding pages: Brucemore's extensive gardens were expanded and embellished by the Douglases after Caroline Sinclair moved closer to town—to the Douglases' own former home. Irene Douglas loved her gardens and frequently sent colorful bouquets to local families and clubs (Bradley Photographics)

see and better understand themselves. The change also brought a need to build touchstones of various sorts to convey the feeling of moss-grown oldness and quaintness. The Victorians were moderns fascinated to look back on old days, but with no desire to resurrect the past. Instead, they wished through it to heighten their feast of the wondrous new, for they believed the present to be much better than what had transpired before. The impulse took many forms: one of them was architecture, and another was pride of ancestry.

Ancestors play a big part in some people's sense of well-being, more so when their lives center in an ancestral home that still shelters a family after many years. This was true of the Chews at Cliveden, that little circle of aunt, nephew, nephew's wife, and progeny. A year before the close of the Civil War, Colonel Benjamin Chew died in Philadelphia. With him went the hate associated with the as-yet unrealized settlement of his father's estate—already twenty years in litigation—and a measure of peace of mind came to Anne Sophia, her brother Henry, and Samuel. There would be no more courtroom scenes or embarrassments in the newspapers.

For Sam, with his strong interest in Cliveden, the death of the difficult uncle turned into something of a windfall. Notices in the press announced an auction of Benjamin Chew's household possessions. Samuel attended the auction and with the help of his aunt identified the furnishings and ornaments the uncle had carried off from Cliveden nearly twenty years before. Sam spent money freely, for he would not have this chance again. Wagons appeared at Cliveden loaded with chests, mirrors, tables, and chairs, which Anne Sophia returned to the places where she remembered they had been.

Also in 1864, during the war, Sam learned that a clerk working in Washington for the Treasury Department had possession of the battle-scarred front doors that had hung at Cliveden during the Revolutionary Battle of Germantown. After his request to purchase the doors was rejected, he began a long, unrelenting pursuit to regain them. Mary Chew, who by then had two children, let pass the condescension of her husband's aunt, kindly omitting mention of the fact that it was her money that was making some of this ancestral revival possible, and still somehow remained a happy wife. She and Sam filled the gloomy stone house with laughter and youth it had not known for a long time.

Once Mary made a brave effort to take control. While vacationing with the children at the New Jersey shore in 1867, she decided it might be best for her to build a house in the city, so she suggested that Cliveden be kept just as it was and used as a summer house, for which it was originally intended. She proposed to add to her new house an apartment for Anne Sophia. In suspecting this might happen, Anne Sophia had begun improvements at Cliveden, notably the addition of a bathroom. She wrote a long letter to Mary, genteel, but firm of hand: "I agree with you my dear Mary in wishing that we could preserve the old house with its uniform architectural arrangements—but finding that Sam wished to have his family more at home—and that your health did not admit of you remaining here in winter without the modern improvements of hot and cold water and a warmer apartment than you have lately had, the convenience of Sam and the children called for better arrangements. I determined to give up my preference in regard to the house, for the sake of accommodating those whose comfort and happiness I have at heart. But if the arrangements I have attempted to make are insufficient—or if you foresee in the future other requirements for yourself and the children, calculated, as you seem to think, to interfere with my comfort or convenience, had you not better say what they are—for it would be a sad disappointment to do the things which I contemplate, and which I fear will require all the funds which I can possibly spare, and then find the purpose unaccomplished—the object unattained—." Mary returned to Cliveden in the fall.

I n most families love for the old homestead was not as all-consuming as at Cliveden, even among some who held on. At Drayton Hall, a house thirty years older than Cliveden, Charles Henry Drayton IV took a different point of view from Samuel Chew. Drayton's ancestral mansion stood in terrible condition after the Civil War, the result of abuse but probably also a decline that had begun well before the war. By the 1870s corn was planted up to its walls, windows were broken out, and there was a general ruinousness about the place. Eventually the Drayton fortune returned again, also from the bounty of the land, by mining phosphate rock for agricultural fertilizer. Charles repaired the mansion, but for a home he built himself a fine, new house in town. He never maintained Drayton Hall lovingly but made the enduring gift of a tin roof. Otherwise he left the house as unchanged as anything can be, and, as Mary

Used part time by the Drayton family, Drayton Hall received considerable repairs in the 1870s and early 1880s. The outbuildings, known as flankers, are probably the only wings the house ever had, but they are gone today (Historic Charleston Foundation)

At Drayton Hall in the 1890s Charlotta Drayton and her brother, Charles, children of Charles Henry Drayton IV, enjoyed their pony cart along sandy roads (Drayton Hall)

Chew had wished for Cliveden, the family used it as an occasional retreat in pleasant weather from the heat of the town.

The preservation of old buildings for their historical interest must be considered a very small feature of the late nineteenth-century mentality. Popular magazines illustrated crumbling streetscapes in Santa Fe, New Orleans, St. Augustine, and Salem; Newport had its venerable colonial houses; and bits of Knickerbocker Manhattan enjoyed brief Victorian sun, before disappearing beneath the brownstone wave. The Victorians, inveterate improvers, never restored much of anything exactly. More often they preferred to replace old buildings with what they believed was better. When they expressed the past in the designs of their buildings, they did so sometimes with abstractions in architecture and interior decoration so subtle that we can barely read them today, a century or more later.

If the war's winds had touched Lyndhurst at all, it was in a different way entirely. The villa was not by that time historic or yet out of style. Philip Paulding sold the estate in 1862 to his father's friend, a prominent Manhattan businessman and machine politician, Robert James Dillon. The estate Dillon received was farmlike, with pastures, woods, and swamps. The slope between the house and the Hudson River was described as "lying wild in a state of nature." It may be that the Pauldings had moved into a cottage on the estate in the last years, keeping the mansion closed up, for General Paulding is believed to have died in an outbuilding. Dillon took special interest in the new house and, flourishing in his wartime business interests, intended to expand the Knoll into a real mansion. He conferred with the original architect of the house, A. J. Davis, to discuss enlargements. They pored over design books by Augustus Charles Pugin, an English proponent of the Gothic Revival.

Whether Dillon actually ever lived at Lyndhurst is not known, but it is doubtful. He kept his residence in the city and also had quarters in Albany, where he was powerful in the state legislature. He did not reduce his political activities during the two years he owned Lyndhurst, and no construction began. A loyal Democrat, he battled the high-riding Republicans on every level, even attempting to sabotage the new Central Park being planned in New York. He paid $65,000 for Lyndhurst and sold it for about that amount two years later in 1864 to a man much richer, at a time when it seemed that the Democrats might win the presidency—and Dillon would have no time for houses.

The new owner, George Merritt, was a bank president, but his recent flush of fortune came from having access to several patents, notably one for a spring for railroad cars that was the basis for his New England Car Spring Company. Enterprise of all kinds was stimulated by the military's needs, and Merritt's wealth had increased to such an extent that, war or not, it was time to have a country house. He followed Dillon's path to A. J. Davis, who produced plans for enlarging the house, closely adhering to the Gothic theme. Davis's notebook suggests that most of the plans, if begun for Dillon, were actually made for Merritt. Twenty-three new drawings were produced in the winter of 1864–1865. Work seems to have been under way in the spring the war ended, when supplies and labor were easier to obtain. Thick new walls of Hastings marble took form in a large added dining room and service wing on the northwest, a porte-cochère on the east, and on the west a monumental new castle tower. The mansion was a villa no longer. It was Merritt who named it Lyndhurst.

Merritt was an inspired gardener, and he transformed Lyndhurst's

Above: This miniature of Lyndhurst's third owner, George Merritt, was painted by Georg Sturm of Dresden. Below: The gardener in Merritt inspired him to create a fabulous glass folly of a conservatory. Regrettably, this exotic architectural wonder was lost in an 1881 fire that toppled its minaret (both, Lyndhurst)

woodland grounds into an ideal landscape, which he adorned memorably with a glass folly. His fancy for the architecturally fantastic he indulged more in this elaborate greenhouse than in his house. The greenhouse was started about 1867, and no American garden house rivaled it. This shimmering, light structure seemed to move, as it reflected the clouds and sun. The greenhouse was larger in outline than the house and contained rooms for tropical plants, camellias, roses, grape arbors, fruit trees, and quarters for staff and male guests, as well as sports facilities. Externally, the architectural idea was to sketch in light materials a sultan's palace—as from some romance—sprawling in long ranges of wood-framed glass wings; from a central glass block rose a hundred-foot minaret, also of wood and glass, ringed by a balcony and crowned by a dome that recalled in shape the Taj Mahal.

"The Merritt conservatory," proclaimed one account of the time, "is in Oriental style, and is the largest in the United States, and cost nearly as much as the mansion. Here may be seen nearly every desirable exotic of the two hemispheres in perfection and tropical fruits growing in the greatest luxuriance; grapes that rival the grapes of Eschol, perhaps." The greenhouse was in full operation by 1870, and one could walk among its palms and orange trees in the dead of a New York winter, while snow fell beyond the glass and ice fringed the eaves. This was the sort of contrast—as between past and present—that delighted the Victorians.

Respect for a symbol of history and famous people captured Edward Fitzgerald Beale's thoughts in the winter of 1871, when his wife, Mary, and he purchased Decatur House in Washington. He had admired the house for its romance during his Washington childhood, and now, returning from California to live part time in the capital, he determined to have it for himself. With it came all of the prestige of its history as well as its prominent position—the long-ago haunt of Washington society in a time so completely cut off by the war that it too seemed in another age.

Eleven years of use by the army as a clothing depot bore heavily on the surroundings of Decatur House in the loss of some outbuildings, including the brick privy and pig pen, and whatever garden there may have been. But the house itself appears to have fared well. For nearly forty years the property had been in the hands of the Gadsby family, early hotelkeepers and slave dealers. To overcome their past, they worked hard out front to place themselves in society. When their own showy period of residence ended in 1844, the house resumed its status as the rented domicile, under Gadsby ownership, of another succession of celebrities, including, most recently, Judah P. Benjamin. Taken over by federal military officials along with other houses on Lafayette Park in 1861, Decatur House served military purposes throughout the war and the balance of the decade. In February 1872 the Beales took possession and called in a team of remodelers.

Edward Fitzgerald Beale, who was fifty in 1872, passed through this book once before, briefly, in California during the Mexican War. He was then glimpsed at the home of Thomas Larkin and knew with some familiarity—and still knew—Mariano Vallejo and his sisters Doña Cooper and Doña Amesti, who had outlived all of the others from the old days in Monterey. At that time he had been a navy lieutenant in his mid-twenties, placed intimate to the action in California's transformation from a Mexican frontier to a territory, then a state in the Union. With Kit Carson he had spied on Mexican troops and carried news to the American authorities, once journeying fifty miles barefoot through enemy lines. He crossed the country overland to Washington twice with important dispatches, the second time disguised as a Mexican *vaquero*, secretly carrying a cache of California gold to show to Congress—a successful attempt, in behalf of the navy, to beat the army's courier to the capital with the good news.

Always a visionary, it followed that Beale was an experimenter. He persuaded the government in the 1850s to introduce camels as beasts of burden to help with surveying parties on the American desert. Camels were imported, and the program was set in motion, but it failed largely because of the interruption of the Civil War. Meanwhile, Beale built a private fortune in ranching. His Rancho Tejon, near Bakersfield, California, consisted of nearly 200,000 acres. It was expertly managed first by Beale himself, then by Indian foremen who reported practically every detail to him. Mary Beale wore a wedding band made of gold that had traveled with him in that navy parcel he carried to Congress. He liked to tell how P. T. Barnum had offered him a small fortune for this personal souvenir, but he had been so in love that he kept it for his bride. The restlessness that sometimes comes with reaching fifty sent Beale from the isolation of the ranch to find adventure in the only other place he really knew and loved, Washington. His friend General Ulysses S. Grant was president. It was high noon in the handful of years Mark Twain was to call the Gilded Age.

Recent scholarship is beginning to clarify the extent of Beale's work on Decatur House and the alterations the house had undergone before him, in the half century since the Decaturs' occupancy. Apparently a sizable amount of neoclassical embellishments had been removed from the drawing rooms on the second floor. Beale undertook a modernization of the two street sides, adding brownstone trimmings and enlarging Latrobe's first-floor windows. Inside, he removed the doors to the main rooms and hung the openings with stylish portières of velvet and tapestry, which not only gave an Oriental flavor but also helped air circulation with the new gravity heating system. Decorative painters created fanciful ornaments, fruit, flowers, and clouds, in sumptuous purples, reds, and greens on the ceiling and probably also on the walls. New parquet floors were installed over the old painted pine upstairs and below; in one of the second-floor drawing rooms, the seal of California was executed in delicate inlays of colored woods.

General Beale, who gained his title from his high position in the California militia and as surveyor general, made quite a handsome presence in Washington. He was a charming if somewhat tough man who liked people

Above left: Edward Beale disguised himself as a vaquero in 1848 to carry news of the gold strike in California. Above right: Walter Sargent's watercolor of the upstairs drawing room at Decatur House captured its appearance during the Beale tenure. Right: General Beale's camels seemed right at home at his Rancho Tejon in California (all, Gordon Beall, Decatur House)

as he found them. All were welcomed under his roof. He liked to recall to guests the stories he had heard as a boy of Stephen and Susan Decatur. And he scattered through Decatur House museumlike memorabilia. In the drawing room he displayed the silver dress sword presented to him by his California militia comrades. A telling portrait showed him as a scruffy young man in his *vaquero* disguise. Camels peered from the frames of two other, larger paintings, and he liked to tell about camels; he greatly admired them and still pampered them as pets at Rancho Tejon. In the remodeled stable he showed his fine horses, as one might show pictures in a gallery. When General Beale decided to try one of his horses in an early-morning sulky clip along the avenues, he might well find himself unable to decline a hell-bent-for-leather race with the president of the United States.

Appointed by Grant as envoy extraordinary and minister plenipotentiary to the court of Austria-Hungary, Beale returned after several years in Europe to take his place fairly much at the head of things in social Washington. The diplomatic scene was one of starched white damask, silver, and crystal, of decorum and rigid codes. Washington was not as formal as most capitals, for the city still had a small-town quality about it. But the Beales were more ceremonial, alas, after their experience among royalty, and they shone in new elegance during Washington's season, December to about Lent. Among the important parties they gave at Decatur House was a reception for General and Mrs. Grant when they left the White House. As was the custom, the press covered the event. Mary Beale, wrote one reporter, wore "a trained toilette of black satin, with point lace and jet trimmings, and diamond ornaments, including a jeweled tiara in the hair."

As noted earlier people in this era were usually more interested in building anew than in preserving the old. They did so in part because the country was rich and filling its vacant regions with new architecture and in part because the triumphant Union saw itself in terms of shiny splendor. But the crash of 1873 that started in Philadelphia and soon hit New York proved that what had seemed golden was really only gilt. Easterners looked back on the years between the Civil War and the crash as one of those closed periods in time. The Gilded Age was not so clearly ended elsewhere. In regions where the panic's ravages were less devastating, some of the character of the Gilded Age survived for many years longer. This was particularly true of the Midwest, where in the mid-1880s a woman in black built a tall brick house, steep of roof: Brucemore, in Cedar Rapids, Iowa.

For the Midwest it was an exuberant time for building. A new and mighty Chicago, rising from the ashes of the old—four square miles of its downtown burned in the fall of 1871—inspired many with the ardor to build. Business people visiting from small towns went home with plans for better shops and houses, fancier signs, gaslight, waterworks, and public improvements. Chicago, rebuilt by 1875 and thriving, was a magnet for the whole Midwest. The greatness of the city had already been well established in a sense by the time of the Civil War. Lincoln had intended to live on Michigan Avenue following his retirement from the presidency, in a house he and Mary planned. In the 1850s and 1860s the railroad service had so favored Chicago that the city became the great hub of transportation, siphoning commerce from older, longer-established ports along rivers all the way to New Orleans.

Both the railroad and the river, but mainly the railroad, attracted two young Scots-Irish cousins, John and Thomas Sinclair, to Cedar Rapids, Iowa, to build a pork-packing plant. This river town, with long-standing connections by water to St. Louis, was approximately equidistant by rail from Chicago and Kansas City, about 240 miles each way. The Sinclairs, heirs of a prominent Belfast businessman, had immigrated to New York in the second year of the Civil War and established a company under the Sinclair name that produced Irish-cured hams and bacon. This venture realized such success that the cousins soon decided to expand beyond just a curing house. They needed a place closer to the source of the pork, realizing that profits would be greater if they purchased their meat on the hoof, directly from the farms.

The Sinclair Packing Plant opened its doors in Cedar Rapids in 1871, the year of the Chicago fire. John Sinclair maintained the office in New York, while Thomas moved permanently to Cedar Rapids. Within a decade they were rich, and the plant had grown, covering sixteen acres with a variety of buildings first in wood, then brick and stone. It was all very modern, but meat packing is not pretty work, and old photographs of the Sinclair Packing Plant confirm that its setting in Cedar Rapids was equally grim, a conglomeration of crowded yards, rambling buildings, and pens.

Thomas Sinclair and his wife, Caroline Soutter Sinclair, who was American born but partly of Scottish extraction, settled happily in Cedar Rapids and produced six children. As Irish-cured hams had made them rich, they made every effort to return something tangible to the community. Thomas sponsored the first water system for the town. A devout Presbyterian, he believed in Christian education and became the patron of struggling Coe College by paying off all of its debts. The Sinclairs intended to stay in Cedar Rapids, and tradition holds that they worked together over plans for a big house. Stylish things interested them. Seen on weekend excursions in the "city," as Chicago was known, or the "town," Kansas City, they were a good-looking couple, she in fine dresses with bustles and lace, her gentle face framed by long, glossy hair done up fashionably *à la grec*. He was what they called in those days a fine-looking man, a compliment not diluted in any way by his burgeoning wealth, and he hid a boyish countenance behind a full beard.

Strolls along the residential streets of Chicago guaranteed excitement to anyone interested in building a house. The rebuilt and booming city provided an introduction to the new architectural styles, with their dark brick and stone, bright tiles, and the intricate woodwork called gingerbread. Col-

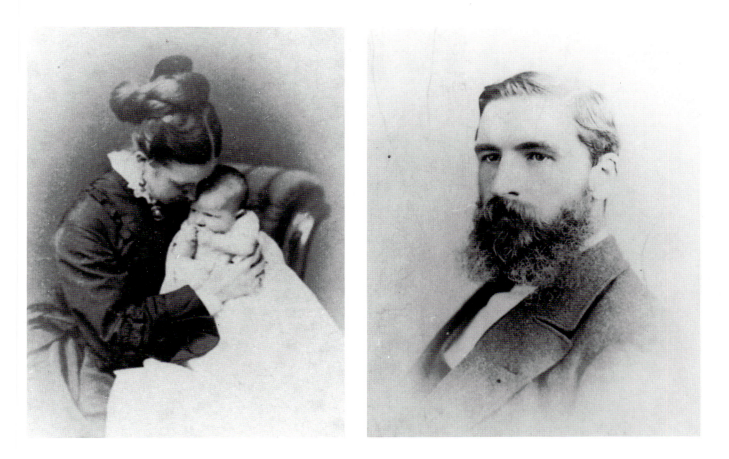

ors of dark red-brown, glossy green, weathered yellow, and sky blue gave emphasis to the nuances of the architecture. The Sinclairs needed a big house for their growing flock. But for Thomas Sinclair the house was not to be. He was killed in a terrible fall at the plant when he was in his thirty-ninth year. The town closed down when the announcement of his death was made. Grief was profound.

The widow was left a rich woman, and the financial picture continued to improve. In her interest, her brother C. B. Soutter assumed a role as one of the directors of the company. At home with her children, Caroline considered her own future, and all signals indicated to her that she must make life proceed as Thomas had wanted it. When her two years behind a veil were over, she met with local architects Henry S. Josselyn and Eugene Hartwell Taylor. Legend preserves her directions to them to build for her "the grandest house west of Chicago." This house, completed about 1886, was to be named Brucemore in later years.

Toward late afternoon, when the workmen were gone for the day, Caroline Sinclair and her children could explore their new premises undisturbed. The house crowned a hill on an eleven-acre site that swept down to First Avenue, somewhat apart from the town. Few trees were present to obscure or soften the massive presence of the building, which, even as a skeleton framework, commanded the horizon in an irregular silhouette, more akin to that of a castle than the square and rectangular residences known thus far in Cedar Rapids. It was in the style called Queen Anne, and as the thick brick walls took shape, the full effect of the mode became evident. The

Brucemore was built by Caroline Sinclair after the death of her husband, Thomas. The two are seen here about 1880, several years before he died (both, Brucemore Archives)

house was meant to look quaint and old, to have the mellow flavor of an English manor built by country carpenters over generations, with no special regard for symmetry. The concept came from England, where the Queen Anne image was historical, recalling architecture before the introduction of building codes—before Victoria, before the Georges, thus the era of "good Queen Anne."

The object of this sort of design, which was fashionable in America in a variety of forms from the 1870s through the end of the century, was not to reproduce or simulate past architecture—as at Lyndhurst—but to evoke its romance and humanity through a creative mingling of historical forms and motifs that made a building exude a mood of oldness and give a physical sense of time gone by. The Sinclair house had red brick walls, pale limestone trim, and windows framed in painted wood. A steep roof of slate covered it, rising, pointing, and sloping in high animation. Ornamental details in tile, molded brick, and timberwork featured the Queen Anne sunflower and a variety of classical decorations rendered awkwardly to suggest the work of a simple housebuilder of Olden Times. In plan its twenty-one rooms were carefully arranged square and at angles, some with alcoves, some odd shaped. The decor was rich in color from paint and wallpaper. The heavy wood doors, the wainscoting, and the great stair were varnished to a shine.

Caroline Sinclair and her children moved in during 1886. Eventually they were followed by fine porcelains, statuary, heavy walnut furniture, and potted palms set in china jardinieres. There were dollhouses, pony carts, and school books, and with time the ting-tang sounds of piano lessons yielded to the smoother strains of orchestras for dancing. Caroline never remarried. For most of the remainder of her life the Queen Anne mansion was to be her home—"the house on the boulevard," it was called locally, and it was considered the best house in town. She also continued her husband's

Brucemore was new and simply called the Sinclair house when this photograph was taken about 1886. The elevated site was rather barren, with no foundation plantings. Red brick, slate, stone, and tile all were combined in a picturesque Queen Anne–style massing of forms (Brucemore Archives)

Above: The Great Hall, richly paneled in butternut, opens onto the library at center. At left can be seen a portion of the Ring Cycle mural added by the Douglases, the house's second owners. Left: The dining room remains much as it was during the years in which Brucemore was home to the Douglas family (both, Bradley Photographics)

charities, and her longing for him was symbolized again and again in chapels, stained-glass windows, and other memorials built to honor his name. Caroline did a good job of raising the children, in carrying out things the way she believed Thomas had wanted them to be.

The Sinclairs' Iowa house was only a dream, and Thomas Sinclair was still alive, in 1876, when the one hundredth anniversary of the Declaration of Independence took the form of a great exposition in Philadelphia, with participants from all over the world. No two people were more delighted than Samuel Chew and his Aunt Anne Sophia. They realized that their beloved Cliveden was one of the greatest relics of that immortal era, and they meant to see that it received its due.

Sam took no active role in planning the centennial celebration—although at Cliveden today he is remembered as Centennial Sam—but Mary, who had ventured out as a social volunteer in Philadelphia, became valuable to the event as a member of the women's committee. It was this group that devised the "colonial kitchen," a popular exhibit that amused everyone with its display of abysmal inconvenience and reminded them, as it was supposed to do, of how much better life had become for women by 1876 than it had been in 1776. At some point after her marriage Mary had become interested in saving Philadelphia's historic buildings for posterity. Now this hobby became an avocation in which she went public. The efforts of Mary's husband and his aunt, however, seem always to have been concentrated on Cliveden. Sam, impressed by the general fascination with history at the centennial, absorbed himself in preparing Cliveden for the world to know through research, art, and the collection of artifacts.

Being so interested in his own heritage, Sam was drawn into closer friendships with such heritage-conscious men as Frank Etting, a founding father of the centennial, people who also gave their leisure to the study of family trees and coats-of-arms. The lord of Cliveden was still an active businessman, but he was less than content with the way the world was changing all around him. In his fascination with genealogy and the historic relics of his family, he was defining himself as an aristocrat. To all of the greatest scenes of colonial heroism he traced one or another of his Chew ancestors. With a side glance toward the Tory shadow over his family name, he showed the patriotism of his deceased forebears. In countless letters to Chews everywhere, he sought information and artifacts. Some of his relatives found his efforts amusing. One cousin responded to his inquiries with a wink at the relevance of genealogy: "[T]his interest is of a rather illusory character, for if we go back to the eighth generation . . . we will find that there were some two-hundred and fifty direct ancestors standing on an equally near relationship to us with the one in whom we are especially interested."

Cliveden may never have looked better than in the 1870s and 1880s. Its grounds were mowed and rolled and planted with specimen trees. Neat

To commemorate the centennial in 1876 Mary Johnson Chew of Cliveden dressed in a colonial-era costume (Cliveden, Inc.)

Above: The parlor at Cliveden, seen about 1895, was furnished with Chew heirlooms and a potted palm, a concession to the age. Left: Sam Chew joined his oldest children about 1871 on the front steps. From the left are David, Anne, Sam, and Bessie (both, Cliveden, Inc.)

flower beds edged the walks. The stone of the house was carefully pointed. Fresh white paint gleamed on the ancient wood trimmings. The roof admitted not a leak. A booming postwar Germantown made Cliveden fit right in as home and museum. Sam acquired more family heirlooms every year, for as relatives learned of his interest, they gave and sold him artifacts in their possession. Cannonballs, antique firearms, old documents, all were placed about the entrance hall. A victory in persuasion was represented in the cannon- and bayonet-splintered battle doors obtained at last from the man in Washington. They were propped proudly against a wall in the hall, not far from where they had hung during the Battle of Germantown.

Everything Sam could do he did to build the fame of his family home. He ordered small engravings made of the house, which he presented to people as gifts, often signing the pictures across the bottom, suitable for framing. Visitors were guided about by him or Anne Sophia, in meticulous detail, through the rooms with their billowy curtains and eighteenth-century sofas and chairs, the white-painted mirrors and the walls hung with family pictures. The silhouette of Chief Justice Chew was a special treasure, and it confirmed the legend that he had a large nose.

Both historians and antiquarians have their moments as dreamers who long for a total recall of a moment in the past, to see it in every detail: to be in the crowd outside Independence Hall on the Fourth of July in 1776, or to be in Wilmer McLean's parlor at Appomattox on April 9, 1865, or even to stand for a moment on a Manhattan street corner on an obscure morning in 1820 would be to see the strange and the different in a parade of everyday life. In Sam Chew's time recapturing the past was the art of the illustrator and painter. As the centennial approached, Philadelphia went through a little renaissance of historical art. The painter Edward Lamson Henry was completing his *Independence Hall* about 1871 for Frank Etting, when Chew met him, and three years later Chew commissioned him to paint Cliveden.

Henry was one of the most famous painters of his time in his specialty of historical scenes. By a careful study of his subjects through documents, artifacts, interviews, and extensive photography of the surviving site, he assembled masses of material and painted his pictures as true to life as he believed they could be again, a historical moment close enough to touch. The prospect of working at Cliveden excited him, and warm letters passed between him and Chew. Wrote Henry: "I dreamed the other Evening of ransacking through your old garret with you amongst old chests, in old presses and like all dreams the imagination ran riot—and I was bewildered with the most rare old costumes, old china, Silver, quaint and singular specimens of Furniture, till they seemed Endless and my wonder was why you never spoke of . . . having such Treasures up there before."

Henry painted three pictures of Cliveden, two of them finished and the third an oil sketch that seems not to have pleased either the artist or the patron. Lafayette's reception represents the leading families of Philadelphia greeting the hero in Cliveden's entrance hall. The more famous of the

Cliveden's front doors, damaged in the 1777 Battle of Germantown, were displayed in the entrance hall for the 150th anniversary of the event in 1927 (Cliveden, Inc.)

Cliveden pictures by Henry, *The Battle of Germantown*, was a staple in textbooks from the 1930s to the 1960s. The third picture, which remained unfinished, shows ghostlike Redcoat intruders floating against the Georgian background of the hall.

These slices of imagined truth had roots deep in the imagination and indeed the soul of Sam Chew. He instructed Henry in every facet of the pictures, from lace cuffs to muskets. For models of costumes and objects, he and Henry ransacked the attic; for accurate representations of people, they called on descendants and copied portraits. If Henry's pictures were his creations, then Cliveden was Chew's. He polished the stone of his heritage until it shone. His affection for the place was different from that of his aunt, who loved Cliveden as a haven. Anne Sophia knew nothing of the world. Sam knew the world very well and how to succeed in it. But like her, he took this house to his heart, and from it received assurance that strengthened him beyond his doors and gave dimension to his life, beyond the pragmatic concerns of business. This seems to have come not only from living at the hearths of his forebears, but also from perceiving the house as a key that unlocked and opened, if only a bit, the closed doors of time. He died at fifty-five, still in his prime, his youngest child only seven, the eldest twenty-five. Everyone agreed that his best memorial was his house.

Jay Gould was painted posthumously by J. Eastman Johnson, based on a photograph taken in the mid- to late 1880s. The portrait hangs in the house today (Lyndhurst)

George Merritt's death in 1873 put on the market a very fine but out-of-style country house that was then among the most costly in the United States. The large and formal Gothic mansion had unsurpassed grace that was not to gain friendly recognition again for nearly a hundred years. By the early 1870s Gothic castles, like Grecian temples, were considered silly and imitative. Julia Merritt was left with a white elephant—indeed, one might say, a herd of them, with mansion, greenhouse, gardens, and farm. When no buyer came forth, she decided to rent Lyndhurst, perhaps thinking that this would capture a purchaser.

It worked. She rented the house in 1878, and the tenant, who purchased it in 1880, was the famous railroad millionaire Jay Gould. He needed seclusion from the city and recognized a bargain. The widow accepted $250,000 cash for the entire property and its contents, and she simply packed her trunks and left. If she ever met the unsmiling Jay Gould, she never said so. At forty-four, in 1880, he was a widely unpopular man, but by the close of the decade he was considered the most hated man in the United States.

Wealth on the scale of Jay Gould's had never been seen at Lyndhurst before. The new owner's fortune was one of the largest in the United States, and at the time of the purchase he controlled more than 10,000 miles of railroad. Within only a few years he gained full control of Western Union, which he founded. Gould was a genius in the art of finance and had created his railroad fortune by cheap purchases of debt-ridden railroad companies, the fallout from the post–Civil War boom. A master of business management,

Top left: Lyndhurst School girls sewed under the shade trees in 1905 (Library of Congress). Top right: Jay Gould's daughter Helen posed with a child at Christmas 1905 (Library of Congress). Above: In the early 1900s Helen Gould and a friend sew in the sun parlor, a space designed for George Merritt that does not survive (Lyndhurst). Opposite: Boys played football on the hilly grounds in 1905 (Library of Congress)

149

he perceived more clearly than most the new economic character of the changed nation; he saw, for example, the need for a national transportation network that would create and serve national markets. Using his railroad combinations as a base, he moved in on Wall Street and with uncanny shrewdness created money earthquakes and financial cyclones with apparent ease. At the young age of thirty-three he was widely believed to have fathered the notorious Black Friday, in 1869, when stocks took a dramatic dive. His ruthlessness became legendary with the Panic of 1873, for which his type was blamed. Society's contribution to the general loathing was to reject Gould's family. While Gould himself did not care, Helen Gould did and was hurt that she and her six children were snubbed. First with the rental, then the acquisition of Lyndhurst, Jay Gould apparently wished to be done with the subject and moved his family away into a pumpkin shell.

The children ranged in age from George, sixteen, to Frank, three. With them came their baggage, little more. They moved in as Mrs. Merritt moved out. The unpopular squire employed an armed-guard patrol to assure the family's safety. He arrived early every evening from Manhattan aboard his yacht the *Atalanta,* was met by a carriage, climbed the hill to the mansion, and spent most of his time working in the small office he made for himself to the right of the entrance hall. Gould devoted long private hours educating himself on various subjects, a custom he had started after leaving school at sixteen. Remaining in his office today are his self-improvement and account books, which he pored over when he had finished everything else.

The mother seems to have spent most of her time with the children. As a couple the Goulds took an interest in their flock of six boys and girls. It was a happy family, thriving reclusively in the shadows of tawdry headlines. They shared many activities at home and traveled together. An old photograph shows them lined up on the lawn at Mount Vernon; Gould was a major contributor to that restoration. The children remembered their father quite differently from history's dark portrait. He was a founder of the Metropolitan Opera in 1883, and his charities were extensive, although quietly distributed. The boys grew up to be like their father, interested in making money, and at moments they too would be money masters. It was with the girls that sentiment took hold.

Lyndhurst was run by a large staff, inside and outside. The maintenance was fastidious even in the remotest part. When in 1881 George Merritt's greenhouse burned down, toppling the minaret, Jay Gould ordered a new greenhouse built to replace it, albeit in a more modern style. The iron skeleton and brick parts of this glass confection survive today. Little otherwise was altered at Lyndhurst. Electricity was installed very late, in 1913, and at various times the heating systems were improved; these changes were of the sort to be expected in the course of using a house. But if Merritt had visited there fifteen years after his death, he would have observed that Lyndhurst looked the same, maybe even better.

For the young Gould boys and girls, Lyndhurst was a fairy castle. They romped its grounds and climbed its battlements and towers. From the tall

Jay Gould's patent Wooten desk, which he used in his New York town house, is now in his office at Lyndhurst. The piece was an adaptation of an old "plantation desk," with pigeonholes and locked doors, that could be hauled around on a wagon to be available for business on the spot. Designed with the railroad in mind, the desk was a portable office ready to be put aboard the train and taken from place to place. How often Gould did this is not known. His desk probably led as sedentary a life as an ordinary roll-top desk (Gordon Beall)

windows of the great second-story room they viewed in sun, rain, and snow the mighty white Palisades across the Hudson. To visit Lyndhurst was to leave behind the city house on Fifth Avenue and retreat to a paradise. Among the six, two would love this place beyond the others. Helen, the third child, moved there at twelve. Anna, age five, worshiped her only sister and followed her in her games. They drove their wicker pony cart deep into the well-guarded countryside. Together they planned dramas to present to their mother and her friends. With Helen, Anna ran down to the dock evenings to greet the *Atalanta*, with its cargo of father and wealthy neighbors, whom by offering rides on his yacht he had gotten to know socially, so different from living in New York. When grown into old age, these two young lives stretched the Gould ownership of Lyndhurst to eighty-one years. On the death of her mother in 1887, Helen found herself its mistress, at the age of twenty-four, helping her widowed father manage the home.

Jay Gould and Anne Sophia Penn Chew died in the same year, 1892, he a relatively young widower, she an old woman. Gould had lived for half of the century, Anne Sophia for nearly all of it. Gould's death brought his family close to chaos over his will but left them rich. Anne Sophia Chew's death made little difference now that Sam Chew, who would have wept for her most of all, also was gone. Both left heirs possessed by the houses in which they had lived, Anne Sophia's tied by family history perceived in glory, Gould's by memories of childhoods spent in unimaginable happiness. Cliveden may have been the first of the houses in this book to take possession of its owner, but there were to be more.

Art Turns the Century

The Victorian period produced entrepreneurs and antiquarians, but it also produced artists. Art, or the spirit of creation, was everywhere. Twenty years after Chicago burned down, the civic impulse that had generated its rebuilding inspired the planning of the 1893 World's Columbian Exposition to celebrate the four hundredth anniversary of Columbus's landing in America. Why in Chicago, who knows? But stranger ideas had landed there, and its supporters lobbied hard for the prize. It is for its architecture that the fair is remembered the most, as the event that popularized the return of recognizable historical styles and stripped away Victorian abstractions. Neoclassical images from the fair were to appear in new buildings for thirty years, and this ideal was to save many an old house from abandonment or demolition, if the house somehow fit the classical picture.

During the several years that preceded the fair's opening, hundreds of artists went to the site with commissions and planned their work. Daniel Chester French, who had been assigned the major nonarchitectural sculpture, doubtlessly walked over the area, envisioning his great statue, *The Republic*, that was to dominate the Court of Honor as the Statue of Liberty does New York Harbor. It was in connection with the fair that he met Henry Bacon, the representative there of McKim, Mead and White, the prominent Manhattan firm that, through its Chicago office, was to build the Agricultural Building. Perhaps with Bacon French polished his concepts for *The Republic, Agriculture,* and *The Triumph of Columbus.*

They were excited by the opportunity presented by the fair and its great promoter, architect Daniel Burnham. Mule teams pulled wagonloads of fill dirt, and armies of laborers graded the site that would be covered with the columned buildings of a temporary dream city in plaster. Already highly respected as the sculptor of Concord's all-American *Minute Man* and a half dozen statues for major government buildings, French was aware of the difference these highly visible Chicago commissions could make in his career. He wanted the work, and the great moment had come when the brilliant Augustus Saint-Gaudens visited him in his New York studio and praised his work. Saint-Gaudens soon selected him for the fair. Henry Bacon, although an important figure on the staff of McKim, Mead and White, was not so near fame's threshold, but he was both talented and ambitious. In the course of their work on the fair and subsequent commissions, French and Bacon became close friends. They collaborated several decades later on the Lincoln Memorial in Washington, Bacon the architect and French the sculptor. But before that, a few years after the fair, they built a summer studio and home in New England for Daniel Chester French.

At this same time in Chicago, as the plaster city rose, Frank Lloyd Wright, architect, had completed a house for himself and his wife, Catherine. He was twenty-two, and his house stood at the corner of Forest and Chicago avenues in the fashionable middle-class suburb of Oak Park. The steep-gabled cottage, its walls and roof covered with wood shingles, neither matched nor severely contrasted with its neighbors, yet it was different from the usual Queen Anne found here in the 1890s. Wright's house would have been more at home in New England, where such designs recalled old, unpainted buildings surviving from colonial times.

The architect's chronic lack of concern over money was already fully evident in the building of the house. He implored his employer, Louis Sullivan, for a loan. Sullivan went with him to see the corner lot, which was part of a small estate being subdivided. It was an "old tanglewood," Wright called it, with overgrown but fine specimens. Apparently as a means of keeping his gifted head draftsman, Sullivan extended the loan, warning Wright that the well was now dry. "I know your tastes . . . no 'extras.' "

Catherine Wright had her way on the Oak Park house in several particulars, but the house was his. It was his first real commission, for as a draftsman he had been, to use his language, merely the pencil for others. The new house bespoke his ideas and the position he believed he should hold socially in the community. He never tired of improving it. Already it could be considered a bit in advance of the usual bungalow cottage. Set up on a terracelike, enwrapping "verandah," covered in part by the deep slope of the roof's eaves, it withdrew from the streets that bordered two of its sides, leaving to public view for the most part only the gable. The lower reaches were embraced in verandah and shadow, and the feeling of increased distance from the streets was heightened by the mature plantings left from the old garden.

The careful manipulation of space inside the house suggested a larger domain than was actually present. Downstairs, the three principal rooms— hall, living room, and dining room—flowed together beneath a heavy, sheltering ceiling, forming a powerful horizontality enriched with polished oak and accentuated by the division of the walls into three parallel strata,

Above: About 1898 Frank Lloyd Wright drew the street front of his new studio, showing the drafting room, reception area, and octagonal library (Frank Lloyd Wright Foundation). Left: Wright posed his family on the porch of their Oak Park house in 1890. Catherine Wright holds baby Lloyd in her arms, Wright himself is seated at right, and his mother is in between (Frank Lloyd Wright Home and Studio Foundation)

Top: The living area has been restored to its appearance about 1909. Left: The master bedroom, with its tray ceiling and stenciling, shows Wright's interest in linear forms. Above: The Wright home presents a decidedly Shingle Style gable to Chicago Avenue. Opposite: The dining room documents the beginnings of Wright's well-integrated personal style (all, Jon Miller, © Hedrich-Blessing)

Above: The library in Wright's studio was an octagonal appendage to the mass of the whole, reached at its single entrance by a narrow corridor; no spot could seem more remote or more tranquil. Opposite: The studio itself is wrapped around and lies beneath a tall open area that terminates at a canopy ceiling with beams that form umbrellalike ribs. Placed around this space on several levels are work areas with drafting tables. Light is abundant and the sense of interaction among the spaces strong, yet the work stations themselves seem very private (both, Jon Miller, © Hedrich-Blessing)

typical of the English vernacular or cottage mode of the time as well as the Queen Anne. A monumental stair rose to a platform, then disappeared behind a wall. In the principal room was an inglenook, a cozy alcove around the fireplace, yet another feature of the cottage mode. Upstairs, two bedrooms and a bathroom served the family, while a third, larger room was Wright's home studio, where he did his drafting—some of it moonlighting—while Catherine was occupied with her pastimes nearby.

So they settled down within a year of their marriage, in the house at 428 Forest Avenue. Six children were born to them. The Wrights entertained and participated in the life of the community, attending Unity Church in a building he was to replace with one of his best designs, Unity Temple. Catherine was a pretty, angelic-looking woman of the domestic sort, who gave her bombastic husband plenty of room, her own interest turning to the children, whom she raised with the freedom of movement and expression popular in theories of the time. She extended her home kindergarten to include neighborhood children.

Wright always spent money freely. His interests expanded into collecting art and crafts. Japanese prints, pottery, Oriental rugs, paintings, and

books he bought as they pleased his eye. "So long as we had the luxuries," he would recall of those Oak Park days, "the necessities could pretty well take care of themselves." He arranged and rearranged his cottage rooms, placing a few blossoms well in a vase, draping a rug at just the perfect angle in the inglenook or on the porch steps, for an afternoon outside. Of this house his eldest son was to remember, "Horizontal lines . . . scattered vases filled with leaves and wild flowers . . . here and there a Yourdes of rare beauty covered the floor. A Persian lantern, samovars. . . . [T]hese made the house that was our home."

Additions to the original house began soon enough, first in 1895 with a grand barrel-vaulted playroom on the east, with its suggestion of the interior of a church. Here the children played every day, and when the Wrights had large parties, it was a splendid salon. Three years later, after his departure from Sullivan's firm, Wright built his studio on the side of the house, with its own commanding facade running powerful and horizontal along Chicago Avenue.

Wright himself grew as an artist as his cottage complex expanded. Work came to him in increasing quantity. He became more determined, more self-certain, more fully developed in his vision of architecture as the years of the 1890s passed by and the new century came on. At the Oak Park house Wright grew from apprentice to architect, and the progress of the man was mirrored in his house, the imaginative yet derivative cottage and at last the assured studio—in the peak of creative vigor, the horizontal movement burst full force, the many shapes inside and shapes within shapes, the control of light, the richness yet containment of decoration, the interplay of materials. This sort of architecture, which seemed to flow in horizontal movement like the Midwest terrain, was called the Prairie Style. Whether Wright invented it, as he would one day claim, or whether he mastered and perfected it is academic. A personal style had emerged in the artist. Here were the characteristics that marked the unmistakable stamp of the first American architect to be celebrated throughout the world.

The World's Columbian Exposition opened and closed as these events transpired in Frank Lloyd Wright's life. Adler and Sullivan designed the Transportation Building at the fair, a mighty polychromatic curtain of a facade encrusted with pattern in relief, Sullivan style, with a succession of arches that seemed to sink to the pillared entrance. Wright assisted Sullivan with the design, and no building at the fair made a sharper contrast to the classicism found elsewhere in the pavilions and halls. It was the classicism, however, that carried the day, a White City of colonnades, porticoes, balustrades, and pilasters, all presided over by French's colossal statue, *The Republic.* The fair came to symbolize everything Wright hated in American architecture, the knell of the Aesthetic approach to architecture and its sacrifice to what he considered imitative. Conversely, for Daniel Chester French, the fair was a triumph.

Four years later, in 1897, when Henry Bacon began designing a studio at French's Massachusetts farm, French was busy with commissions great and small. As Wright had come of age as an artist, so had French, in a different frame of time, on a different wave, on common ground only in the kinship of purpose most artists share. Largely because of the great success of his allegorical works at the fair, French was able to move from the historical work that had first brought him to public notice and devote himself to the expression of abstract ideas through human figures. His approach had roots in the American neoclassical tradition earlier in the century. Yet French had parted from that manner of art, which, like that of his contemporary Augustus Saint-Gaudens, sought the ideal not in beauty but in the truth of reality. He did not adopt the distortions of Michaelangelo for his figures; rather, in pose and facial expression, particularly of the female form, he rendered his themes through believable human forms.

French was in demand, and he employed a staff of about six at his home and studio at 125 West Eleventh Street in New York. Like Wright in Oak Park, French had expanded his premises there, to work on the monumental statuary he created for public buildings. For several summers before and after the fair, French and his wife, Mary, liked to follow those New Yorkers who could afford it and escape to cooler, less crowded places. They were an amiable couple, she a native of Washington, D.C., and also his first cousin. Of the many interests they shared, one was country life, another history. They tried to suit themselves as summer folk in practically every part of his native New England. French disliked the distractions of fashionable art colonies, although they visited Saint-Gaudens pleasantly a couple of times in Cornish, New Hampshire, and French shared his studio there in the summer of 1891. It became clear that the increase in commissions called for a working retreat. A sculptor, unlike a painter, could not simply pack up his tools: he needed a permanent place to house big things. A farm seemed the answer.

In 1896, looking at properties near Stockbridge, Massachusetts, they saw possibilities in the Marshall Warner Farm, which had mountain and valley views. Mary French liked Stockbridge; just the year before she had told her husband, "I don't know what you're going to do, but I am going to live here." The artist now looked for the money. Fairmount Park in Philadelphia had commissioned a statue of General Grant, and the officials there agreed to extend a $3,000 advance. Daniel Chester French paid cash for his farm.

Back in New York he made his plans for the farm he later called Chesterwood. The old house they would repair and use as their residence. In idle times in the winter of 1897 he haunted antiques and junk shops, buying this and that for the farmhouse. After the Frenches moved to the farmhouse with their only child, Margaret, they papered and painted in the

Top: Daniel and Mary French posed for snapshots at Chesterwood on a June Sunday in 1907. Above: In 1922 French was working in his studio on a bust of the inventor Ambrose Swasey. In the background is the seven-foot plaster cast for his seated Lincoln, unveiled that year in the Lincoln Memorial (both, Chesterwood Archives)

163

Top: French's studio opens onto a fountain and semicircular seat where he liked to sit (Paul Rocheleau). Above: The studio piazza overlooks the house (Robert Lautman). Right: Andromeda is shown on the railroad tracks French specified for his works (Paul Rocheleau). Opposite: The studio entrance is on axis with the garden's grassy path, which extends into the woods (Paul Rocheleau)

spring and summer. For a studio French made temporary use of the barn in 1897, but he was eager to have a studio built exactly to his needs. He called on Henry Bacon, who had left after nine years with McKim, Mead and White and formed a partnership with James Brite. The studio may have been Brite and Bacon's first commission. French, wanting the studio as near perfect for his purposes as possible, made very careful specifications. When it was warm enough in April 1898, work began on the studio. April 1898 was also the month the Spanish-American War began. Public emotion was high. The Frenches were at first reluctant, then in support of the declaration of war against Spain, but they could have been on another planet from the clatter of current events.

The new studio was sited where the old barn had stood, and French carefully preserved the barn on a different location. A long, airy piazza gave the studio its only full view of Monument Mountain. Other than a studio, a different use for the structure can hardly be imagined. The interior was dominated by the large work room, which opened onto the piazza and out to the mountain. Entering the building on the other side, through the reception room, one was presented with a retreat warmed by a corner fireplace. Paintings and casts hung on the walls. Comfortable chairs were arranged about, and French installed an eclectic array of antique tables and stools, together with chests of costumes for his models. A draped alcove sheltered a Pompeiian couch. In the reception room, the family sat and talked, clients were poured tea, and through a large opening the great studio was revealed in splendor beneath a fall of natural light from the skylight and windows above.

The studio was a place of hard and concentrated labor of mind and muscle. It was a simply finished interior. Heavy wooden modeling tables served the sculptor. Railroad tracks passed to the outside through double doors twenty-two feet tall, allowing French to move his clay and his plaster figures, regardless of size, on a handcar into the open air, to be seen outdoors as they were intended. The railroad also helped in loading crated marble statues on trucks to take them to the railroad station for shipment.

French pencilled on a shelf in his casting room, "Moved into studio July 11, 1898." He was pleased with his rural workplace and was to cherish for the rest of his life the six months he spent there each year. French produced in his Chesterwood studio some of the most popular sculpture we know today. His earlier *Minute Man*, installed near the North Bridge in Concord in 1875, already was the classic representation of the patriotic volunteer (it would be used on defense savings bonds in World War II). French's seated *Lincoln* was born here in the spring of 1915 in a fist full of clay and grew over five years, through a series of alternating clay and plaster models, into the colossal masterpiece in marble that was unveiled in the Lincoln Memorial in Washington in 1922.

Chesterwood developed as a gentleman's farm in which Dan and Mary French took pride. They constantly devised improvements: stone fences, new fields, outbuildings. An ornamental garden was begun as soon as the

Opposite above: This room in the studio was where French cast clay models into plaster (Paul Rocheleau). Opposite below: At the entrance to the studio is the reception room, which French filled with his eclectic collections. Clients were brought here when they called at Chesterwood (Robert Lautman)

studio was complete. Margaret French remembered her father as a serious gardener who "felt about gardens pretty much as he did about statues—that if you got your essentials right, your foundations, in other words, if your skeleton and your bones were in the right places, then the chances were you'd have something worth looking at."

By the turn of the century the Frenches had to admit that the old farmhouse was inadequate for their needs. They had company every summer, and the tiny bedrooms and single bathroom off the dining room kept everyone crowded and uncomfortable. Henry Bacon replaced the old house with a suburban-looking stucco house of the colonial type with Georgian details that French seems to have liked for his antiques. Ample of windows and gleaming hardwood floors, the new house contained a parlor copied exactly from one French had known as a boy in his family's New Hampshire homestead, and French placed in the same location his grandfather's old sofa. The sculptor had the mantel and wood trim carefully removed from the original farmhouse parlor during demolition and reinstalled in his new study behind the stairs, a bit of the soul of the old brought to the new. For the hall columns beside the stair French designed capitals with ears of corn, recalling the famous ones by Latrobe in the U.S. Capitol. In a Venetian glass bowl on the dining room table he floated three fresh pink roses in season, an effect he had seen and liked many years before at Alma-Tadema's London studio.

The new house fairly well completed the complex that we know today at Chesterwood. Dan and Mary French never tired of improving their farm. Although he sculpted and she wrote plays and stories, they were not opposed to taking up the hoe and rake themselves, and they often did so in the cool of early evening. As Margaret grew up, they carefully monitored her education, giving her every encouragement to become an artist herself. On summer days they were likely to hold teas and occasional receptions to introduce completed sculptures.

The sculptor and his friends performed *tableaux vivants*. Other artists came to call. Isadora Duncan was both a guest and a youthful friend who valued French's opinions on her costumes. She liked to perform for her hosts. Mary French recalled that one time, "we dressed her up in wreaths of flowers and pieces of drapery, and tried all kinds of experiments, and some of her poses were certainly very beautiful. . . . As she danced upon the upper terrace of the garden, with her long fragile figure, red poppies in her hair, her fleeting motions, she seemed like a Greek figure come to life." Margaret's friends came to an annual costume ball at Chesterwood, before autumn brought a return to the city. Gypsies, Bluebeard and his harem, Dante and Beatrice, kings, and queens assembled in the studio, where to the music from a three-piece orchestra they danced until midnight supper. "It is as beautiful as fairy-land here now," wrote French one late spring, "the hemlocks are decorating themselves with their light-green tassels and the laurel is beginning to blossom and the peonies are a glory in the garden. I go about in an ecstasy of delight over the loveliness of things."

The sculptor's daughter, Margaret French (right), and her friend Marjorie Lamond dressed as the goddess Diana and a bacchante, respectively, for Margaret's second annual costume ball in August 1913. French himself designed the costumes. The pillar is one of a pair that forms a gateway to the Woodland Walk at the north end of the garden (Chesterwood Archives)

If French had an antiquarian side, it was directed more toward objects than buildings. He liked the idea of old buildings more than the old buildings themselves and even distrusted the old as being impossible to adapt to modern purposes. His residence at Chesterwood, with the tone of a rambling old house, is wholly of his time. This he preferred. No more perfect an antithesis to him could be found than Paul Kester, French's contemporary and also an artist in New York. As the Frenches were moving into their new house in 1901, Kester purchased for himself down in Virginia the sagging, paintless, vacant mansion of Woodlawn. He did not want to change much of anything.

Slender, boyish-looking Kester was, at thirty-one, one of the leading playwrights on Broadway. His avocation, it might be said, was old houses, and he loved them all the more for their cracked plaster and creaking boards. He is seldom remembered, because his plays were mostly adaptations of popular novels—vehicles for well-known performers who were more the play than the play itself. Only through the careers of Lily Langtry, Marie Tempest, Annie Russell, Margaret Anglin, and Julia Marlowe does his name really ever come up in the history of theater. "He wrote in an era of stars," recalled a colleague, "when fashioning parts for them appeared to be the dramatists' job rather than making good plays."

It was a time when New York theater was considered the best in the world. Six months was a good run for a play on Broadway, and Kester might boast two or sometimes three plays at once. The era is remembered in bright lights for a youthful Ethel Barrymore's opening in 1901 in *Captain Jinks of the Horse Marines*; Maude Adams and Sydney Brough appeared in J. M. Barrie's *Quality Street*; Eddy Foy was in *The Strollers*; George M. Cohan sang and danced *The Governor's Son*; Richard Mansfield played *Beau Brummell*; and Ada Rehan, who had come out of a long retirement, captured the season in Paul Kester's *Sweet Nell of Old Drury*. Rivaling it a little later was a second Kester play, *When Knighthood Was in Flower*, based on the novel by Edwin Caskoden and featuring Broadway's current favorite, Julia Marlowe.

Earnings from *Sweet Nell* probably provided the $8,000 he paid for Woodlawn. Unoccupied for thirteen years, the house had suffered careless ownership by a residential development company and severe damage to one wing by a storm. Kester ordered the chimneys cleaned out and some walls painted. He had the ruined wing rebuilt, larger; then, concerned by the imbalance it created, ordered the other wing expanded to match. A mishmash of used bricks was laid in the walls, so they would look old. His housekeeper, Mrs. Andrews, inventoried his odd furnishings: there were large rugs "fit only for the walls of museums; millions of books, pictures, and engravings . . . portraits, of unknown ladies and gentlemen of any era. . . ." The portraits, a silent chorus in period costume accompanying the performance of his home life, surveyed mahogany sideboards, dining tables, towering canopied beds—all trophies from antiques hunts in New York. Wrote one of his guests, "Paul loved the country with an abiding passion for old houses . . . but he never could afford to restore them."

Shortly after he bought Woodlawn, playwright Paul Kester autographed this photograph to his assistant, George Middleton, who helped him with The Cavalier *(Billy Rose Theatre Collection, New York Public Library for the Performing Arts)*

Like Wright's home and French's retreat, Kester's Woodlawn was first of all a place to work. Kester settled in and concentrated on his plays. In addition to his mother, Kester's brother, the scratchy-voiced, sickly Vaughan Kester, was also there, constantly at work writing articles and western novels. While he was getting settled at Woodlawn in 1902, Paul Kester had another hit on Broadway with Lily Langtry, the Jersey Lily, in *Mademoiselle Mars*. This success helped him pay his carpenter and painter, but so much of his money was taken up by railroad tickets, hotel expenses, and the high costs of hospitality that he never had any to spare. Moved perhaps by his southern surroundings, Kester undertook in 1902 the task of adapting George W. Cable's novel *The Cavalier* to a play for Julia Marlowe. She was devoted to him, not only as a friend, but as the one who had turned her stage career from small salaries in Shakespearean tragedy to comedy's big salaries in *When Knighthood Was in Flower*. Now the star hesitated. She considered herself in trouble, and before she could even think of signing to do *The Cavalier*, Paul must bail her out.

Marlowe was appearing in a new play, *Queen Fiametta*, based on Christopher Marlowe's salty original. The play had brought her some adverse criticism, because audiences were not pleased that she would portray a loose woman, and Julia Marlowe was aware of the importance of loyal fans. How could she leave and save face? Kester's solution was daring. He wrote a solemn press release, proclaiming that Julia Marlowe had suffered a nervous breakdown. The understudy would take her place. Through the crowd of spectators gathered outside her hotel, Kester escorted his charge, her face veiled, supported at the arms, to a cab and onto the train. Once aboard, in the drawing room Kester had reserved, she tore off her veil and sat down to a hearty dinner. As New Jersey flew past the window, she and Kester congratulated themselves on the little lie that had freed her from *Queen Fiametta* and that, in the newspapers, put her away to rest in some obscure Virginia hot springs resort no reporter could ever possibly find. They disembarked in Alexandria and rode by surrey out through the mellow autumn farmland to Woodlawn.

Mother Kester had everything in order for them—abundant country cooking, peace and quiet. In one of the downstairs rooms that looked toward Mount Vernon and the Potomac, they set up shop to recreate Cable's *The Cavalier*, the story of a southern belle—a beautiful, black-haired southern belle—who falls in love with a Yankee spy. One of the sets even was to resemble the interior of Woodlawn. "We worked like Trojans," remembered Kester's assistant, a young man named George Middleton. He especially labored, spending long hours at the typewriter, taking dictation from Kester, or polishing dialogue while Kester and Marlowe walked together on country roads, talking and planning, then returning to criticize what Middleton had done.

But Middleton was living a dream, no matter the hard and thankless work. Just out of college, he was working for one of Broadway's best writers and writing for its most popular star. "At night," he remembered, "I would

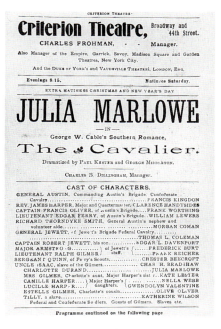

Above: The playbill for The Cavalier featured the popular actress Julia Marlowe. Opposite: Marlowe starred on Broadway in The Cavalier, written by Paul Kester at Woodlawn (both, Theater Collection, Museum of the City of New York)

walk out alone to register all I was learning. Once, I heard her singing. She was trying the scene we had written: she, a Confederate woman, was singing to a dying Union prisoner who loved her "The Star Spangled Banner." In the darkness I heard Marlowe's voice thrilling with the song and the emotion of the scene. When it was over I ran to her room with tears in my eyes. I kissed her hand. As I said, I was twenty-two. She didn't mind."

In New York the manager teased the public with stories of Marlowe's "great improvement" and even suggested a "possible return to the stage." At Woodlawn Marlowe took plenty of exercise and ate like a farmhand, while Kester coached her in her lines as the southern belle. Just before bedtime, the household was received into Marlowe's bedroom, the one to the left at the top of the stairs, where she had arranged herself luxuriously against a bank of pillows and beneath a crimson down comforter, her hair unfastened and brushed long. As her visitors took places quietly in chairs in the room, she took from her table a book, perhaps a novel or a play, or one of Vaughan Kester's stories, or a poem by Paul, and filled the cool October nights with her wonderful voice.

Then the schedule arrived in the mail. Rehearsals were to begin in mid-November for an opening in New Haven in mid-December, then on to Broadway by Christmas. Wrote assistant George, "[A]s soon as we came to New York, the idyll was over," and sadly, "I almost ceased to exist." The news coverage never mentioned Middleton in its celebration of Kester and the resurrected Marlowe. But thanks largely to Paul Kester, the assistant received half of the royalties, and when he picked up a program at the theater, "My name was there! Paul Kester and George Middleton! Nothing else mattered."

Kester stayed on at Woodlawn until 1905, when another house caught his eye in an advertisement, an English mansion named Angill Castle. He purchased the property fully furnished and sight unseen for $25,000, the exact figure he received for Woodlawn in one payment from Elizabeth Sharpe of Wilkes-Barre, Pennsylvania. The wealthy Sharpe, heir of large coal interests, was ready for a change of scene. For many years she had stayed at home, lovingly supervising the care of invalid parents. Relieved now from this responsibility by their deaths, she had been scouting about in warmer climes, but not too far away, for a farm with a colonial house she could restore. Kester knew her slightly and had shown her Woodlawn first simply to satisfy her interest. When the castle came up, he got in touch. He named his price. As soon as the deal was closed, he was making arrangements to sail to England.

Elizabeth Sharpe delicately pronounced the house, to her eyes, in disrepair. Kester's offer to loan some of his antiques she accepted, then she opened the doors to carpenters, plasterers, painters, plumbers, electricians, and the delivery men from appliance companies, who furnished her kitchen anew. Old Mrs. Kester and Vaughan bought nearby Gunston Hall, George Mason's home, and moved there. Paul made an exit like a character in one of his plays, suitcase in hand, off to a new adventure, frail of planning, strong on impulse, as becomes both artists and stars.

Four years later yet another artist's departure took place. By 1909 Frank Lloyd Wright was considered moderately famous—not fame like that of Daniel Chester French or Paul Kester, but he was sought after as an architect in Chicago, especially of private houses (he designed some twenty-five in Oak Park alone) and the attention pleased him greatly. His lecture "The Art and Craft of the Machine," delivered at the Arts and Crafts Society in Chicago, meeting at Hull House in March 1901, was widely read and translated into several foreign languages. *The Ladies' Home Journal* illustrated one of his Prairie houses, a mode in which he had become more assured and more flamboyant, and by 1909 he had been featured in *The House Beautiful* and the professional magazines *The Brickbuilder, The Architectural Review,* and *The Architectural Record,* all of which represented enviable recognition in his field. Only recently, new commissions began to come to Wright from outside the Midwest, in Canada, Tennessee, California, and New York.

But while his involvement in his work intensified, and his own sense of purpose in improving architecture increased, he became dissatisfied with his domestic situation. He was annoyed that Catherine paid more attention to the children than to him or his art, and the noisy, rollicking children themselves gave him no peace. He felt trapped. Escape came soon enough in a love affair with an Oak Park matron, Mamah Borthwick Cheney, who was his client and also a club friend of Catherine's. Wright had designed a house for Mr. and Mrs. Edwin Cheney a short walk from his own home and studio. Mrs. Cheney, so unlike his own wife, professed to be a free spirit, spoke of free love, and was much interested in matters of the intellect. When her affair with Wright began is not certain, but it was heated to a frenzy by the fall of 1909. When Wright left for Germany and Italy to supervise the preparation of a portfolio of his work, she joined him.

Except for a brief return, Frank Lloyd Wright was never again to live in Oak Park. Catherine Wright could not accept the fact that he had abandoned her and would not agree to a divorce until 1922. The love affair became newspaper copy of the most lurid kind, for the press, fresh from reporting on the sex-drenched scandal of Stanford White's murder, had an appetite for architects. Catherine gave a news conference, accompanied by her minister, and defended her husband. She extolled his great gifts as an artist and said that she was convinced that he was innocent of wrongdoing. Eventually the news cooled down, and for a while the peering eyes were directed elsewhere. Wright subdivided the studio into living quarters, so Catherine could rent the house for income. He believed that he had satisfied his obligations. Then, as though free as a bird, he took Mamah home to Wisconsin, to a beautiful gardenlike hillside across the river from Spring Green, where, seemingly with no money to his name, he established himself on his family's land at the first place he was to call Taliesin.

America Joins the World

City people's wish for air and room started a popular movement toward open spaces around the beginning of the twentieth century. All that was really new about this idea was its widespread adoption and the variety of forms it took, particularly in middle-class suburbs. For rich people the notion was an old one. Cliveden was built as a country retreat in the eighteenth century. Lyndhurst followed in the 1830s. And at the turn of the century, the ideal of country life took on a historical tone with the restoration of old farms and plantations as well as the construction of new ones that suggested established estates, American, English, or European. Even at a time when nearly universal interest was turned to improving the city—the 1893 Chicago exposition was meant to suggest a model "city beautiful"—the draw of green pastures led to a flourishing period of country living and interest in country life; on a certain economic level, this preoccupation consciously imitated what was then happening in Edwardian England.

Country places of this sort are more akin to gardens than farms, gardens in two different senses of the word. On the first and most obvious level, the owners of country

Opposite: In the library of his town house in Washington, Woodrow Wilson spent many hours with his memories. He had taken the nation to and through World War I, but in retirement, aging and ill, he felt discarded by the citizens he had served (Ping Amranand)

❖

Preceding pages: A dramatic feature of William and Agnes Bourn's garden at Filoli is the High Place, suggesting a ruin, where a semicircle of column shafts, divested by time of their capitals, has been linked by rich, green walls of entwined yew trees. The ghostly vine, trained on chains swagged between the columns, is wisteria, only beginning to leaf out in this early spring view (© Alexander Vertikoff)

places all planted ornamental gardens. Daniel Chester French at Chesterwood, for example, created a rather small formal garden as an intimate forecourt to the entrance of his studio, with a semicircular marblecement seat, a central fountain, and a peony-bordered path rising from this straight as an arrow away from the studio, over a close-cropped lawn into the embrace of a natural forest of hardwood trees, floored with lovely, plumelike New England ferns. In a second, more abstract, use of the term, *garden* describes the perfection of the country places themselves, in cases where the "manor house" stood on enough land to be considered a farm. Sometimes they were working farms, but only in name. They never supported themselves entirely from the marketing of their bounty but were brought to a high state of agricultural improvement for the sake of pleasure and appearance, through the expenditure of what might be called external resources. They were, therefore, in themselves gardens.

Central to one version of the country ideal—although not a signature like the garden—was the historic house, rich in its evocation of human handiwork and a simpler, greener past made credible by time. Elizabeth Sharpe opened her tall windows and drank in the sweet-smelling hay and wheat that clothed Woodlawn's hills. She delighted in telling her guests of a ghost rider she had seen on a ghost horse racing up Woodlawn's driveway, circling the boxwood ring she had planted out front, and vanishing toward Mount Vernon. It had to be George Washington—who else? Proud of her farm, she declined Paul Kester's offer to buy it back when he became bored with his English interlude. Kester rented the house for a few summer months while she traveled; he always said that selling it had been a mistake.

Sharpe's interest in Woodlawn made her curious to know more about its history. In Mount Vernon's records she learned about the girlhood of Nelly Custis and the visit of Lafayette. Her work on the large brick house was unending. Antiquarian through and through, she went on trips to country sales with her friends and patiently awaited the fine old Virginia drop-leaf tables of walnut that turned up on the block in line with hay wagons and milking equipment. Where a fireplace mantel was missing, she wanted the perfect specimen in its place. Woodlawn's great windows she draped in damask and chintz and, in summertime, theatrical gauze. As a means of better understanding her house, and preserving it on paper, she employed an architect to measure it exactly and provide scale drawings for her. Not many years before, some measured drawings had been done for the Chews at Cliveden, although for other reasons.

At Woodlawn, both Waddy Wood and Edward Donn, Jr., architects in Washington, accomplished tasks for Elizabeth Sharpe, including a revision of Kester's work on the wings, to make the new bricks on the added parts match the old, original bricks. If Kester had liked things to look patched, Sharpe did not. The architects implored her to reduce the wings to their original size and erase Kester's clumsy enlargement, but she refused to surrender the interior space. She considered herself as a restorer, in spite of keeping the new attic rooms in the wings. Dan Tyler, the carpenter at Mount Vernon, saw to it that her projects worked out well. He built numerous cupboards, benches, doors, and other essentials. Set in mown fields outlined with whitewashed fences, Nelly Custis's house was no longer forgotten.

In 1900, the year before Paul Kester bought Woodlawn, William and Anna du Pont ended their search for just the right American estate with the purchase of James Madison's Montpelier. To protect the buyer from a high price tailored to him, the actual transfer was made to du Pont's secretary, King Lenning, who spent $74,130 in assembling six properties to make a total of 1,240 acres. Over twenty years du Pont increased Montpelier's acreage to nearly 3,000. He and Anna, both in their late forties, were returning to America from a five-year residence in England, essentially a social exile necessitated by their divorces and marriage. Life in Wilmington was still uncomfortable for them: if they returned there, the children Marion and Willie, six and three, might grow up exposed to unkindness.

The du Ponts appreciated the fact that the house had an important history and thus credibility, and not the least an aristocratic tone even an Englishman would accept. Du Pont was himself an active businessman, the owner of an agricultural fertilizer company and several other enterprises. His wealth was not new, of course, but its immense scale was new and had nothing much to do with his own business. The fortune he enjoyed was family money, acquired when the venerable gunpowder producers of Delaware became the suppliers of munitions for the government during the Spanish-American War. There were more genteel ways to get rich. With the financial alteration came a new level of leisure that was to spawn in the large family several generations who built English-like images of landed aristocracy, the characteristic counterbalance to an industrial tinge.

Montpelier had been fortunate through the Victorian decades not to have suffered extreme neglect or radical alterations. About the time of the Civil War someone had cut the front porch steps and floor back behind the row of tall columns, to protect it from rotting. The columns, made of plastered brick, were reshaped to reach to the ground, and the portico took on the character it has today. Dolley Madison's long, one-story colonnade still stretched across the back just as it had in her day, some sixty-five years before. A series of wealthy owners in the 1880s and 1890s were sympathetic to the authenticity of the place and had taken good care of it. For several years before William du Pont came along, apparently it had stood empty.

The du Ponts planned to live at Montpelier full time. For their purpose the rambling old house, oddly divided up inside, was too inconvenient, small, and plain. Whether or not they hesitated before ordering a total revision is unknown. But in 1901 and 1902, by chopping out and building anew, the house lost most of its identity in plan and was swelled externally into a huge, awkward parody of its former self, with great wings spreading out hotel-scale from the original columned block. Architecturally, Montpelier had never been perfect. It could be argued that it had grown even in Madison's time from an unadorned brick house into an ill-proportioned sham of a temple, plastered to hide the seams. Furthermore, by the close of 1902, Theodore Roosevelt's remodeling of the White House might be called up in favorable comparison—although it was true that Roosevelt had preserved the exterior. As for the du Ponts' viewpoint on this, the encapsulation of historically significant structures was done all the time in nineteenth-century England, from which they took inspiration, so their decision at Montpelier cannot have given them much pause.

At the remodeled Montpelier a rural routine was created that was a happy charade of life on a large, self-sufficient farm. It was a wonderful garden of that kind. William du Pont made his estate a model farm, investing money wisely in good advice, the latest improvements, and an army of employees. Weedy meadows became beautiful pastures, against the backdrop of the Blue Ridge Mountains. Anna enjoyed her enlarged old house, although only one room of the Madison residence, Madison's study, really survived mostly intact. She ordered elaborate plasterwork for some of the ceilings and arranged in a drawing room at the rear of the house some fashionable reproduction *belle époque* furniture that she purchased in France. When a cousin brought a charming legend to her that Lafayette, when he visited Montpelier in 1824, had stepped off and laid out a garden for Madison, based in design on the old House of Representatives chamber

William du Pont, seen here with his son, Willie, was an ardent Anglophile like his wife, Anna, and converted Madison's home into an American version of an English estate (Raymond Woolfe Collection)

in Washington, Anna du Pont ordered plans drawn to revive and improve the estate's old surviving garden along the lines of its supposed origin. The result was the present formal, terraced garden walled in clipped boxwood, resembling in outline the great assembly room that was burned by the British in 1814.

Montpelier was to thrive as the home of the du Ponts for more than eighty years, almost the same number of years the two generations of Madisons lived there. They filled it with their possessions and occupied it completely. Their stables were among the most famous in the United States. Eventually a racetrack joined the barns, paddocks, and rows of stalls that were the accouterments of horse sports. The estate had everything to hold anyone who loved country life, with no reason to fear a crop failure. Montpelier even had its village, with a railroad station. Of all of the Virginia estates reestablished during this period, Montpelier was, in total, the most magnificent.

A restored Oatlands was not so splendid or extensive, but its purchase in 1902 by newlyweds William and Edith Eustis created a stir of interest in Loudoun County when word got around about who had bought the old Carter place. The young Eustises lived in Washington, across the side street from Decatur House, in the sprawling, exotic mansion of his grandfather, the art patron William Wilson Corcoran, who had raised him. Edith Morton Eustis was the daughter of Levi Morton, former American minister to France and vice president under Benjamin Harrison.

Billy Eustis was heir of the Corcoran fortune, which was another war fortune, only in this case from banking during the Mexican War in the 1840s. His father, George Eustis, like his mother's people, the Corcorans, was a Confederate sympathizer and was appointed to the mission to England that included James Murray Mason. Captured at sea with Mason, he was imprisoned with him in Boston for a time, before joining his wife and father-in-law in France, where he remained until his early death, a widower, at forty-four. The three children, including Billy, were sent to America to live with their grandfather in Washington.

Billy Eustis had grown up with a silver spoon in his mouth, attaching himself to all gentlemanly pursuits. He was a fine athlete, notably a horseman, and was founder of the Loudoun Hunt. After his marriage he wanted a house of his own, where he could develop his stables. He and Edith combed the country for the right place and at one point considered building, but they liked the feel and charm of old houses. Edith finally saw Oatlands and was pleased with it. They purchased the house and sixty acres and within a few years added about a thousand acres.

The former occupants of Oatlands vacated the house to make way for the Eustises. George Carter II, son of the builder of Oatlands, and his wife, Kate, had returned to the farm during the Civil War with his mother,

William Corcoran Eustis's portrait at Oatlands shows him in uniform during World War I. With his wife, Edith, he revived a dying Oatlands and made it into a country retreat of just over a thousand acres (Oatlands, Inc.)

Top: Edith Eustis visits her terraced, box-wood-lined flower garden at Oatlands in later life. Above: Her portrait by Carolus Duran was painted in Paris before her marriage (both, Oatlands, Inc.)

Elizabeth. They stayed on. Hard times in postwar years forced them to sell off land to raise money to live and pay taxes. His brother, Ben, filed several suits to try to get part of George's land, and the cost of this litigation nearly ruined them both.

In the 1870s George and Kate, in a desperate financial state, opened Oatlands as a summer boarding house, attracting people from Washington and Baltimore. Guests at Oatlands rode out to Leesburg on the train, where a driver and surrey met them and took them to the farm for an unhurried, well-fed country vacation. With their guests the Carters played masters of the mansion, their parlors furnished with heirlooms, with oil-painted portraits of kin of the mighty King Carter looking down from gold-leaf frames. It was hard work, however, keeping things together behind the scenes. Several black families, remains of the seventy former slaves who had come home after the war, helped keep up appearances for paying company. George and Kate counted their take and paid salaries to their workers. She raised turkeys and he learned a bit about repairing things himself.

The boarding house was a success, but by the late 1890s, when the Carters and their helpers were too old to continue, they stopped and the old house sank into neglect. Finally George and Kate, simply tired out, sold their mansion to a real estate speculator, who never moved in, and five years later he sold it to the Eustises. The Carters relocated down the hill in an old cottage of unknown origins, where they hung their ancestral portraits and settled in happily. Kate Carter died as the work of restoration began on her former home. George lived, very poor, for another twenty years, moving off the property and selling the surviving acres of his land. He died in a Leesburg nursing home in 1926.

Meanwhile, the tall, columned house shone anew, its stucco walls painted butter yellow, its elaborate neoclassical trim snowy white. This restoration was a gentle effort, respectful of the house as it was. Inside, temporary partitions built to accommodate the boarders were torn out, new bathrooms installed, hardwood floors laid, new electrical wiring added, a modern steam-heat system put in place. But the handsome interior spaces were not distorted or enlarged. For furniture the Eustises used what they could spare from town as well as, over time, trophies from auctions and antiques shops. Under the supervision of Billy Eustis, the barns and fields were improved, and year after year the acreage increased in beauty. Fall weekends, groups of pink-coated horsemen crossed Oatlands's green hills, performers in a country pageant of imagined tradition that had extended from New York and New Jersey at last to Virginia to such gardens as these.

Another aspect of the country life movement in the early twentieth century was the creation of entirely new estates. The king among these was George Vanderbilt's North Carolina chateau, Biltmore, but there were others. Whitemarsh Hall, near Philadelphia, now gone, was the closest America ever came to recreating a stately Georgian country house; and there is Filoli in Woodside, California, twenty-five miles south of San Francisco. This house was built between 1915 and 1917 by William Bowers and Agnes Bourn, their first permanent residence since they fled their San Francisco house in the earthquake and fire of 1906.

Fifty-eight in 1915, Bourn had been an heir at seventeen to his father's gold mine, the Empire Mine in Grass Valley. He prevailed in that business through sheer grit, leaning on the advice of his cousin George Starr, a mining engineer. He extended his business interests into public utilities, notably the Spring Valley Water Company, which had a monopoly on the supply of drinking water to San Francisco. At business management he was exacting to the penny. But risk taking held such magic for him that he once lost a winery and vineyard at poker. Too hasty a judgment of his character along these lines, however, somewhat misses the man.

An English education, and a fascination with the vanishing aristocratic life of Europe, made William Bourn something of a paradox among the usual businessmen of his time. A man of tremendous physical vigor, he traveled abroad with some frequency and, if not exactly a student of art and architecture, developed an interest in and appreciation for both, because they represented a manner of living that seemed to him the natural reward of wealth and power. His tendency toward the intellectual might suggest a man who liked to be closeted away on occasion, just to think. To the contrary, he was always alert to control all that was around him. When his daughter Maud in 1910 married Arthur Rose Vincent, a British subject and

William Bowers Bourn, photographed about the time he began building Filoli, was a shrewd businessman who took daring risks. An admirer of French, English, and Irish country life, he created such an image, regionalized, in his Crystal Springs Lake estate south of San Francisco (Filoli Center)

career judge in the judicial office of the British Foreign Service, he forbade her moving to Zanzibar, where Vincent had been appointed to His Majesty's Court. Vincent resigned. The obedient couple was rewarded with Muckross, an 11,000-acre estate in County Kerry, Ireland. For all of the distance this put between father and daughter and son-in-law, it never relaxed Bourn's domination over them.

Bourn did not have his way, however, in 1915, when he decided to build an estate on the banks of Crystal Springs Lake, which was the source of water for the Spring Valley Water Company. By law private ownership was not allowed on this vital resource for the city, and even Bourn's power could not move the officials. Instead, he purchased 1,800 acres with views of the lake and started Filoli, the home he envisioned as his castle and paradise for the rest of his and Agnes's lives. The name was a hybrid he created from the first two letters of the words in his motto: "To Fight, to Love, to Live."

House and garden were begun about the same time. The architect was Willis Polk, who had worked for Bourn on two houses previously, one a massive neo-Georgian pile in San Francisco and the other a mountain lodge of stone that recalled smaller seventeenth-century manor houses in England. Filoli was one of the largest private residences Polk ever built. The architect was a sometime hunting companion of Bourn and a personal friend, although this relationship soured in arguments over the high costs of the new estate. Polk designed only the mansion, not the garden or outbuildings. Bourn remarked that the site reminded him of Ireland, so he wanted a country house that was an Americanized version of those Anglo-Irish houses he had enjoyed there, including his daughter's house at Muckross. From nineteen sketches presented by Polk, Bourn selected the one he liked the most. The result was a house of forty-three rooms, with 36,000 square feet of living space. Conceived in the Beaux Arts ideal of past styles renewed, it was essentially Georgian, very much pared down to a stark, almost Tuscan simplicity, with a tile roof that seemed right for California.

One entered the house from a large, paved forecourt, flanked by the wing for the kitchen and service areas and the ballroom wing, which was left unfinished for about five years. The interior featured a row of large, tall rooms along the rear. A system of corridors provided ready access for servants to all of the rooms but, curiously, precluded their passing from one side of the house to the other except by crossing the main drawing room or going outside. The rooms were rich in paneling, carved stone, and plaster decoration. English and European antiques and reproductions were used as furnishings, selected for their scale to the rooms, no room too full, none barren or even sparse.

Filoli does not have an especially memorable interior, for all it cost. It is too big and so overworked as to lack freshness, perhaps the result of excessive refining and replanning and meddling on the part of the client. But Filoli was from the start more a garden than a house, and what developed in its garden was to make this one of the finest private gardens in the United States. Bourn envisioned the natural view to the southeast as the backdrop

Above: Agnes Bourn posed at Filoli in 1918 (Filoli Center). Opposite above: The view of the house from a terrace reveals the strict geometrical pattern of the gardens, a foil to the brilliant color and lushness of the plantings (© Alexander Vertikoff). Opposite below: Weeping cherry trees and tulips show brightly against the dark green of boxwood and yew (© Alexander Vertikoff)

of hills, lake, and trees for his garden. The idea is reminiscent of the garden scheme of Bantry and other Irish country houses. His house was not sited to face the view, but the garden, extending from the side of the residence, reached toward the panoramic sweep of landscape, which today is obscured by trees on the property between the garden and the lake. An early garden design was tossed out in favor of one by a California designer, Bruce Porter, who had worked on interiors many times for Willis Polk. Porter successfully produced a concept of a garden of dreams, cooled by pools, colored by flowers, and abstracted by architectural shapes in living green.

The features of the sixteen-acre garden in Bourn's day were the great Irish yew and holly trees, many of them slipped from old plant material at Muckross in Ireland. As at Muckross, the yews and hollies were sheared into formal columns and walls and grew dense and compact. For the selection of plants for Bruce Porter's plan, and for the coordination of garden color, Bourn turned to Isabella Worn, the leading floral decorator of the Bay Area. She had delighted him many times with the bouquets she placed throughout his house for parties. At Filoli she devised color schemes for the vast parterres, the terra-cotta vases, the allées, and the terraces, an artist with her floral paints. Her taste guided Filoli's designs for nearly forty years.

Although it was not open to the public, Filoli's garden was one of the wonders of California. Those privileged to see it wandered in awe along its stepped walks to the spectacular view, then turned back to see the garden all at once, growing complex and varied down the long slope to the place where the mansion seemed to hide beneath its deep roof of red-orange tiles. It was a garden rich in the abundance of its plants and dramatic in the high state of control it imposed on nature. Bourn, the host, invited house parties to Filoli with frequency. Young men challenged to tennis matches learned the virtue of losing rather than arouse his anger. He who was forever young mingled with his guests and carefully planned their total enjoyment of his paradise. Long California evenings were spent beneath paper lanterns strung over the walks of the garden, in the fragrance that never seemed to leave Filoli.

The United States entered World War I as Bella Worn was planting the gardens for the Bourns. Europe's conflict was now ours—only our cause, understood as grander than theirs, was to save democracy in the world. Few understood the extent of change the war would bring to their lives. One ardent patriot was William Bourn, and he turned his remarkable energy to the war cause. At Chesterwood the last summer costume ball was held in 1916. In Margaret French's photo albums, the beaux dressed the year before in summer white have reappeared in army uniforms. The old summers were gone. Daniel Chester French contributed large sums of money to the English and the French. Billy Eustis volunteered and left Oatlands to fight. At Montpelier, William du Pont sent

Opposite: An iron gate leads from the sunken garden to a walled garden at Filoli (© Alexander Vertikoff)

money to England for the war cause. A Browning machine gun was brought out from Wilmington, and he and Willie tested it with vigor; the windows rattled and bullets riddled the garden wall.

The realities were hard. A few years after the war's end, feelings were still so strong over its conduct and conclusion that, for some, anger boiled beneath the surface. Once optimistic, Americans had watched the forces of improvement turn to the destruction of humankind itself. Many—perhaps most—mistrusted the war-inclined nations of Europe and harkened to Jefferson's view long ago that Europe was degenerate. Woodrow Wilson's presidency closed sadly for the man who had led the nation through the war. Victory's aftermath proved empty for him, thwarted by politics in the realization of his ideas for assuring the perpetuation of peace. The president became a tragic figure, his health broken, seeming the more old and pitiful beside his younger companion, Edith, wife of his later years. He had his detractors, to be sure. When in 1920 his friends set out to purchase a house suitable for his retirement, Edith Wilson told them she wanted Woodlawn. Elizabeth Sharpe dismissed them coldly. Wilson and his international ideas, said she, posed the greatest danger to the security of the nation since the Revolution. She would see Woodlawn torn down before she would allow that man to live there. Woodrow Wilson's friends left quietly.

There were other houses. While house-hunting one day, Edith fixed on a tall, Adamesque town house at 2340 S Street in the northwest section of Washington, D.C., just off Embassy Row. It was about five years old, built originally for Henry Parker Fairbanks, and its location made better sense than Woodlawn's for the Wilsons. The house was constructed from designs by Waddy Wood, who had worked earlier for Elizabeth Sharpe. He was the premier residential architect of Washington and a minor master in building new houses inspired by the Georgian and colonial vernacular of the eighteenth century. Edith Wilson, back at the White House, told the president she had found the place, and a few days later he surprised her with the deed. Ten friends, including the millionaire Bernard Baruch, had made the new home possible. Baruch purchased the vacant lot next door, to assure the Wilsons' privacy.

To the red brick house Edith Wilson moved furnishings that had been in her own house on Twentieth Street and on the second floor of the White House, into which Wilson's late wife, Ellen, had moved their belongings from Princeton seven years before. The new house was ample in size, rising three stories above a service basement with kitchen, pantries, and servants' hall. Wood had designed it with every detail for modern convenience, an attribute perhaps summed up best in the third-floor linen room, with its neat cabinets, drawers and bins, and high windows for borrowed light. The formal rooms on the main floor included a drawing room and a dining room, as well as a large library. Most striking of all on that floor was a diminutive solarium on the back overlooking the leafy, elevated garden.

In the last months of Wilson's presidency, from January until March 4,

Edith and Woodrow Wilson moved their possessions from the second floor of the White House to 2340 S Street in Washington in late February 1921. Their new home was in Embassy Row, where the neighbors were foreign officials who admired the former president's internationalist views (Woodrow Wilson House)

Above left: Based on the porch and the windows, the street front of the Wilsons' house appears to have been influenced by Robert Adam's eighteenth-century Adelphi in London. The tall second-floor windows light the drawing room (Gordon Beall). Above right: Former President and Mrs. Wilson depart the house in 1922 to attend the dedication of the Tomb of the Unknown Soldier, attracting a crowd (Underwood and Underwood). Left: The kitchen preserves the Wilsons' original range and equipment. Light floods in from an areaway outside the windows (Gordon Beall)

The Wilsons' dining room is seen through the doors of the solarium. Edith Wilson's portrait by Seymour Stone, painted in the Green Room of the White House, hangs over the fireplace (Erik Kvalsvik)

1921, Edith Wilson and the White House staff labored to prepare the house. The woodwork was given a shiny coat of ivory-colored paint. Edith favored decorating with soft tones of grays, yellows, blues, and ashes-of-roses. Some rooms were papered. Everything found its place, and it was a great mix of things. On tables in the drawing room, in front of the great window that looked out on S Street, silver-framed autographed photographs of kings and queens lined up with those of Wilson's daughters by his first marriage. On the wall opposite the fireplace Edith hung the beautiful Gobelin tapestry that had been a diplomatic gift to her. Mementoes of her trips with Wilson to the Versailles Conference found places of importance, including the furniture from her shipboard suite. Upstairs, a

sunny bedroom on the back of the house was fitted up for the president. When its windows were opened, breezes blew in, beyond the organdy curtains. It was restful and private and reminded Wilson a little of their bedroom at the White House.

On Warren G. Harding's inaugural day, the Wilsons departed the White House to attend the inauguration at the capitol. They returned to the new house, feeling at first a little blue, as the car rolled along, then laughing heartily between themselves, and finally, as the car entered S Street, moved almost to tears that a crowd awaited them, applauding. Through the doors of 2340 S Street Woodrow Wilson passed from the public life he had known. It was one of those moments that mark the end of an era.

Above left: The drawing room contains furniture from Edith Wilson's previous home in Washington and the Wilsons' quarters at the White House. The Gobelin tapestry, folded to fit a smaller wall here, was a prized possession of Edith Wilson (Ping Amranand). Top right: Wilson's bedside table still contains objects he used in his last years (Gordon Beall). Above: From the solarium on the back of the house french doors open onto a deep garden (Gordon Beall)

This portrait of Frances Adler Elkins by Gene McComas was her favorite of herself and always hung in her dressing room at Casa Amesti (Sydney H. Kalmbach, Casa Amesti)

he war was over less than a year when Casa Amesti in California and the Shadows in Louisiana were purchased and restored by two people who probably never knew each other but who were kindred spirits indeed. Frances Adler Elkins was twenty-eight when she acquired Casa Amesti in Monterey, and Weeks Hall, great-grandson of David and Mary Clara Weeks, was the same age when he undertook the restoration of the Shadows in New Iberia. Each saw in the houses works of art to be brought from the dark into the light. In their houses each created a haven from the changes the war had brought, and their creations, with time, came to possess the creators themselves.

Casa Amesti, like at least half of John Cooper's adobe house across the street, had remained in the same family; slightly before and during World War I it was rented for use as a boardinghouse by a flower-loving French woman. She had a taste for plants. An old photograph of her garden, on the side of the house, shows neat beds filled with blooming things. Her extension of the garden beyond the old adobe wall to where the sidewalk should be aroused protest in the city government, but she prevailed. Property lines in Monterey were rambling things anyway, so who was to give a reason that she could not plant where she pleased?

When it came on the market in 1918, Casa Amesti was not, therefore, a ruin but a mellow old house that attracted Felton and Frances Adler Elkins to make this their place in the California sun. The Amesti heirs had hoped to dedicate the house as a retirement home for Roman Catholic women, but so complex was the estate's entanglements that the house was put up for sale. There being no need for negotiation, Felton Elkins paid $5,000. Auctioneers called for the family furnishings that were still in the house, including thirty-six matched chairs that had lined the upstairs *sala grande*, added when the house was given its second story about 1853. Whether the furnishings were offered first to the Elkinses is not known, although likely, and likely declined. She had other ideas.

A restoration of fact was not what the chic, artistic Frances Elkins was interested in. She was not one to labor under the weight of fact—a look at her personal manner of dress, the way she wore just the right scarf, carried the perfect handbag, her gloves, her jewelry, her elegant carriage, all revealed that she had too many ideas of her own to allow the past to possess her. Like the Victorians a generation before, she wanted only a mood of the past, not a reproduction. Her past was to be composed of relics, chief among these the house itself. She called in as architect her brother from Chicago, David Adler, the principal residential designer in the city's fashionable suburbs. They had been raised in Minnesota and from childhood had shared a love of artistic things. He was a master of the art of creating small, formal houses adapted to the customs of modern living, but visually traditional, and is remembered today as a better residential designer than his Main Line and Long Island contemporaries who were on occasion challenged by him on their own turf.

Frances Elkins wanted the look of the old house preserved, with the addition of all of the modern conveniences known in 1918. To achieve this effect, Adler had to dismantle a large part of the interior and put it back together again, providing chases for wires and pipes and bathrooms and closets, without distorting the original appearance of the house. Items removed were simulated by replacements, so the appearance of old adobe prevailed, with some embellishment, in added woodwork, mantels, and other ornaments that heightened the provincial qualities of the rooms through contrast. Sixty-five years had passed since the Mexican house had been Americanized with its upstairs additions, and no part of it was a hundred years old. Yet it was a classic expression in vernacular architecture of California in Mexican days, a theme that had already been seen in new California houses before the turn of the century. Revising a historic house of this sort was something new, yet the presence of the old walls and floors, the 1853 stairs, balconies, and enhanced trim gave a romance to Frances Elkins's house that a new house never could have.

People are usually drawn to old houses by the aura of the history they represent—not necessarily the facts in detail, but the romance, which may be largely fiction. If for the last half century the sparks for these fires have come largely from the movies, in Frances Elkins's time they came first from literature, then from architecture. The adobes of Monterey, with an appealing innocence of architecture, represented to the eye of 1918 a varied "colonial" California culture that mingled such characters as *rancheros* and soldiers, priests and Indians, with all manner of seafaring folk and crown and later Mexican officials, who moved in and out of the scene. David Adler and Frances Elkins felt safely within the bounds of the idea to enhance Casa Amesti with a cosmopolitan flavor, while playing up the existing background of simplicity. Even as the work was beginning on the house, they plowed under the French woman's flower garden and redesigned the walled space as an Italian garden with clipped hedges, a fountain, and lines of whitewashed flower pots.

The house was completed by early 1920. Frances Elkins began her work of furnishing. Her husband bankrolled the antiques buying and let it grow large scale, and her brother made constant recommendations. Santos from Spain, silk cushions, painted French and Italian armchairs, a candle-burning chandelier, rich mahogany tables, antique prints, and handsome old volumes bound in leather were some of her purchases. Stereopticon slides she took of the finished rooms in the early 1920s show that the main rooms today are still about as they were then, evoking a cosmopolitan culture in a simple architectural shell. The rooms are carefully arranged settings, a plan that extends to the walls themselves, which are decorated with groups of pictures and objects. Block-printed linen, faded chintz, white and bright azure paint, all combine with the dark, bare, waxed boards of the floors. Antiques of all kinds—American, French, English, Italian, Chinese—contribute to the evocation of a lost age of sailing ships and a wild and beautiful, unspoiled California of old.

The first-floor library at Casa Amesti is to the right of the street door and was created by Frances Elkins and her brother, David Adler, from an Amesti bedroom or parlor in 1919 (Jim McHugh)

The sala grande was the parlor in the days of the Amestis. It was added in the 1850s, when the house was given its second story. Originally it seems to have been a barren room, its walls lined with mahogany side chairs. Frances Elkins made it her living room, its architecture embellished by David Adler, its contents a mixture of antiques that caught the eye of its artistic owner in various parts of the world (Jim McHugh)

When Frances and Felton Elkins divorced in the 1920s, and he returned for a time to Philadelphia, she soon ran through what money she had and necessarily turned her hobby of decorating into a business, joining that relatively new legion of merchandisers, the interior decorators. She opened a shop in Monterey. Among her projects was the interior of the Royal Hawaiian Hotel in Honolulu, where traces of her work remain in deep tropical colors and old-looking ironwork and tiles. She resisted her brother's entreaties that she move to Chicago, and she always spurned that other lure, New York. California was fine for her. There were annual buying trips to Europe and good living at home in a domestic scene that her daughter, Katie, remembers as characterized by good food and wine: "My mother was *not* the family type." Eventually David Adler joined her for long visits at Casa Amesti, occupying a small room with an alcove bed near the large *sala* upstairs, and Frances decorated it with cabinetlike closets with black-painted glass in the doors—just the sort of closets Don Jose Amesti might have built long ago, had the Spanish used closets.

In Louisiana, Weeks Hall fell in love with his family home. At the age of twenty-five, he purchased his aunt's share of the Shadows, becoming the sole owner for the price of $7,500. Three years later, in 1922, with some inheritance in his pocket, he was ready to do whatever it took to restore the house. The Shadows stood intact, its columns facing the street along which automobiles now rambled, its rear looking out over Bayou Teche through a jumble of outbuildings, a slumped-over rain cistern, and chicken yards. Weeks Hall was the sort of fellow who flourishes in good and constant times; indeed, had there been no world war, he might have slid on from boyhood to youth and into a successful life in art. The storms of his times so tossed the craft of self in which he sailed that his path was interrupted. After brief service in the navy, he tried to pick up the pieces. He had already studied art briefly on a scholarship at the University of Pennsylvania. Able to recoup scholarships offered to him before the war, he lived in Paris and London for two years.

Back home, Hall returned to the Shadows. He had not liked the wider world and never returned to it; he made the Shadows a substitute. His letters from 1922 through the balance of his life show remarkable candor and continuity in his attitude. His was not an existence forced on him, but one of choice—a comfortable, perfectly natural choice for him. He reflected on his upbringing in a household in which there were "no other children." His had been "an adult childhood," lived in New Orleans and briefly in Kansas City, where his father died young. As a teenager he followed his parents and aunt around in the magical, memory-shrouded world of the Shadows.

"There were the usual potted-plants and much of the aroma of the nineties," he wrote. "The house was neglected except for the gutters and the slates and there was no plumbing and no electricity." In the yard he found bare, packed earth beneath the spread of great live oaks that must surely have shaded his ancestors. A "half-dozen Camellia trees" were scattered about, "and a clump of Bamboo opposite the Southwest pillared front. . . . *There was not an Azalea of any sort on the place.*" The Shadows lingered in his mind, and it beckoned to his heart. He determined to restore his house, and keeping it became the focus of his life.

Weeks Hall engaged the services of architect Richard Koch of New Orleans, who was probably the only architect in Louisiana at the time interested in restoration. Koch was fascinated. Great care was taken to leave the house in as original a condition as possible. A careful examination of the bayou front showed clearly that the house originally had a recessed rear porch or loggia, but it was left as it was because, wrote Hall, "It must have been closed with brick almost immediately after the house was built, for there is very little difference between the two sections of brick, in color or in quality." The only real alteration Koch made, according to his client, was to balance the lattice rain screen that protected the outside stair on one end of the front gallery with the same screen on the other side. He also replaced some flooring and exchanged flooring in one room for that in another. Bathrooms were built inside existing spaces. The house proved sound and needed little serious repair. Its preservation as a specimen of early Louisiana architecture was important to Weeks Hall.

While the work was going on, Hall explored his domain. The house was entirely furnished, the attic filled with storage. Some forty trunks were opened to reveal old clothing and hundreds of letters and family papers. Portraits leaning against the wall were stripped of their newspaper wrappers and revarnished by the former art student himself. Chairs with broken legs were brought down for repair. In the rooms 1890s wallpapers were peeled away. The parlor's Victorian overmantel was taken down, freeing the funereal black-marble mantel selected by David and Mary Clara Weeks from its walnut burden. The walls were painted for the most part that yellowish southern white called magnolia white. Hall had the broad board floors sanded and waxed, rejecting the idea of carpeting them or covering them with straw matting, as they had always been.

It was completed at Christmas 1922, the same house, only edited of its clutter of generations. The rooms were, by comparison, rather bare. Practically everything in them was original to the house, from the china on the sideboard to the big high-post beds and armoires upstairs. Uncurtained windows at first and the lightness of the walls contributed to the bareness, yet in their decorative self-consciousness the rooms were akin to those of Frances Elkins at Casa Amesti. Her furnishings were in great numbers, acquired at antiques shops. His, fewer in quantity, were for the most part heirlooms of the house and its past. Both had undergone a strict process of selection by their owners before being admitted into these sacred realms.

Weeks Hall, finished with his house, began the transformation of the garden. For many years he performed a strange exercise in saving old plants and increasing their number through propagation. "It is so important," he wrote, "to develop what is *already there* and to preserve it." What he wished to achieve first was to screen his house from the noisy street. He separated the clump of bamboo, freeing it from whatever container had kept its natural aggressiveness at bay, and planted it along the inside of the sidewalk and the sides of his four-acre property. Bamboo grows fast. Within a short time, the Shadows was obliterated from the street, except for the tips of its dormers, the ridge of its slate roof, and the chimneys at each end. "The tall and dense Bamboo hedge," wrote Hall, "is very necessary to the preservation of the atmosphere of the place."

The brick outbuildings between the house and the Teche, including the original kitchen, smokehouse, slave quarters, and privy, were pulled down carefully, to save their bricks for use in garden walks. To the rear of the house, up to the high bank of the bayou, he built his "circular garden," for which Richard Koch designed in 1928 a green latticed gazebo, a cocktail place overlooking the lazy stream. Southeast of the house the "square garden" contained the old camellias and many new ones, together with hundreds of azaleas, planted forestlike. Statuary from an abandoned sugar plantation provided images in marble, set on plastered brick piers.

But the most effective feature of the garden was the way in which Weeks

Top: The Shadows was photographed in the 1930s by Frances Benjamin Johnston, enveloped in Weeks Hall's landscaping (Library of Congress). Left: Weeks Hall posed in the 1940s with his English setter (Shadows-on-the-Teche). Above: Determined to document the house, Hall shot virtually every inch of it, including the attic with its Shadows-like dollhouse (Shadows-on-the-Teche)

Hall created a sense of distance between the house and the street, when there was relatively little by actual measure. He set at each end of the bamboo wall plain, narrow gates made of boards that gave access to the property from the street. They admitted callers into small areas enclosed in green, like outdoor vestibules, from which gravel walks twisted snakelike to the house, thickly bordered by aspidistra leaves; walls of tall plantings screened the house from view as one progressed along the walks, so that it came in and out of view as one walked closer, drawn farther from the town and deeper into the enchantment of the garden.

In August 1922, as the Shadows underwent its repairs, William Bowers Bourn suffered a stroke at Filoli, and this was followed in October by a worse stroke that distorted his appearance and confined him to a wheelchair. Youth was not to be eternal after all. With his nurse he took air in the gardens. The gardeners and servants were ordered to hide themselves when he appeared, lest anyone seem to be watching him. He wanted no sympathy. Even Agnes could not change his attitude about what had happened to him, although she tried and was the only one at Filoli with whom he would spend time. He built an ironwork porch, wholly private, from which he could see Spring Valley Lake. His years were lonely through the 1920s except when Maud and Arthur and the children came to visit. Then in 1929 Maud died suddenly of pneumonia in New York on her way to Filoli from Ireland. Bourn had loved his daughter more than anything else. On his orders she was buried on a hill at Filoli.

Struck hard by Maud's death, Bourn sold all of his businesses, conducting these transactions sight unseen, through agents, never leaving home. The parties, dinners, and balls continued at Filoli, Agnes Bourn in attendance. In 1926 the Bourns privately published a book of poems, *Some Favorites*, that had sweetened and inspired their lives. Copies were presented as gifts to special friends. When Agnes became ill in 1932, she no longer presided but remained upstairs with her husband, while the parties continued below. Bella

Filoli's new owners, Lurline and William Roth, had an abiding interest in the continuation and improvement of the gardens of their California estate. Their twin daughters, Lurline and Berenice, dined with William Roth aboard one of their Matson ships in the 1950s (Filoli Center)

Worn planned the occasions, and she or a Bourn relative received the guests. At Filoli today is a surviving invitation to a merry "Drunks' Dinner" in honor of the end of Prohibition in 1933. Across the bottom is printed, "Mr. and Mrs. Bourn, being sober, will not be present." Nor did the entertaining stop until the death of Agnes Bourn in 1936. He followed six months later. They were buried on the hill beside Maud, and a Celtic cross of stone was commissioned to mark the graves, to be carved with the words "To Fight, to Love, to Live," from which Filoli's name had been taken. The mason mistakenly omitted from the slogan the word "love."

William Bourn made no provision in his will for the preservation of Filoli. This omission seems odd, because he and Arthur Vincent had given Muckross and its lands to the people of Ireland in 1933 in memory of Maud; but for Filoli no such perpetuation was assured. His grandchildren sold it largely furnished in 1937 to William and Lurline Roth, she the heiress of the Matson Navigation Company and he its president. The Matson line carried freight and passengers between California and Hawaii. Among Matson and Roth interests was the Honolulu Oil Corporation. Filoli was in rich and, indeed, loving hands. The Roths enjoyed country life. They kept extensive stables, for both saddle and harness. And they maintained and enlarged the gardens, keeping Bella Worn on to direct the gardening operations as she had for so long. Lurline Roth's affection for gardening centered particularly in camellias. Worn brought them in by the truckload, planting them carefully, with an eye to every nuance of color.

Time thus passed through the 1920s, the Depression years, and to World War II. For the most part the houses in this book were better off than they had been, a fact that makes them exceptional. Montpelier, which became the home of William du Pont's daughter, Marion, was maintained to perfection and even enjoyed a certain tinsel glamour during her brief marriage to the movie star Randolph Scott, a local boy and old friend, before his permanent return to Hollywood. Margaret French Cresson, after the deaths in succession of her father, her husband, and her mother, kept Chesterwood in memory of the happy times she had lived there.

Belle Grove was purchased and restored in the late 1920s by Francis Welles Hunnewell, a Harvard botanist, who had Washington architect Horace Peaslee remodel and renovate the house as a base of operations for his researches on plant life in the valley of Virginia. On Elizabeth Sharpe's death in 1924, Woodlawn was sold, its contents auctioned off by her heirs from Pennsylvania; walnut, mahogany, china, and silver, the bounty of years of antiquing, went on the block. Some of the furnishings were purchased by the new owners, Senator Oscar Underwood of Alabama and his wife, Bertha, who moved there in 1925. Underwood, a fierce opponent of the Ku Klux Klan, had run against Woodrow Wilson for the

Senator and Mrs. Underwood arrive at the White Honse in 1925, the year they moved to Woodlawn (Library of Congress)

Top: At Brucemore daughter Barbara Douglas (fourth from the left) and her friends climb a fence about 1914. Above left: Irene Douglas (left) displays volumes from her book bindery. Above right: The children's room about 1910 was a secure haven (all, Brucemore Archives)

Democratic nomination in 1912 and had turned down Wilson's offer of the vice presidency in 1916. Brucemore, in Iowa, changed hands early in the twentieth century, when Caroline Sinclair traded it in 1906 to George Bruce Douglas for his house nearer the center of town. Douglas, a businessman heavily involved in the Quaker Oats Company and other businesses, including a starch works, doubled the acreage. Irene Douglas built greenhouses, planted flower gardens, and added a book bindery.

By 1925 Frank Lloyd Wright's Oak Park home and studio had been sold, later to be subdivided into rental units. His home had first been rented out for income shortly after he returned to this country in 1910, and the studio was converted for his family's use. Meanwhile, he had moved to Taliesin in Wisconsin. The architect's love affair ended in tragedy in 1914, five years after he left Oak Park, when Mamah Cheney and her children were murdered by a crazed servant who also set afire Wright's first Taliesin. After a long seclusion, Wright emerged at the head of his field in the late 1930s.

During the Depression he turned his energies to inexpensive housing for the middle class. His new concept was the Usonian house, a residence for Everyman—affordable, designed with style, and built using "natural" finishes, such as wood, and the best modern building materials, such as concrete. Usonian houses made a strong and optimistic architectural statement in Depression times, when the financial state of things disturbed Wright not as much as F.D.R.'s big government remedies, which he loathed. Fearing the loss of the individual in so much change, Wright offered his architectural solution in a new sort of building for democracy.

One of many Usonians he designed was a small residence in Falls Church, Virginia, for Loren and Charlotte Pope, a house that preceded Wright's own home and studio into the protection of the National Trust. The Popes admired Wright's ideas from his books and asked the architect to design a house for their family of three; Loren was then a young reporter with the *Washington Star* and later was to become well known as an educational consultant. Built on the Popes' one-and-a-half-acre lot outside Washington, D.C., the house was completed in 1941, a few months before Pearl Harbor. The cost was about $6,000, not cheap; the same figure would have purchased a roomy Cape Cod or more than one average bungalow. From the street the Popes' house hugged the ground in Wright's trademark horizontal flow—a trim, refined container made of cypress, left to weather, slumbering among the trees, fallen leaves, and ferns of its forest site. On the back or private side, it awakened to daylight and the landscape with large openings of glass casements and french doors; light entered more subtly through bands of decorative cutout openings whose almost Pre-Columbian shapes dapple with light the diminutive, cavelike volume of the living room and corridor.

Of the other National Trust houses, the Popes' house relates most to Wright's Oak Park home and studio, of course, but the linear character of its plan distantly reminds one of that same quality in Lyndhurst's plan; a closer kinship to Brucemore cannot be overlooked, in its powerful embodiment of the vernacular flavor—without the specific theme—and the aesthetic effects so potent in the Queen Anne of Wright's formative years. For all of the future they seemed to represent, Frank Lloyd Wright's houses had a reassuring feeling of tradition. But to live here one had to live according to the dictates of the building; it was no house for a large family or a string saver. Its personality as a place was so dominant, however, that to one sufficiently fond of artlike and unusual houses, the shortcomings were minimal.

Around the time of World War II, Loren Pope and his son, Loren, Jr., sit on the screened porch of their house in Falls Church, Virginia. The chairs were designed by Frank Lloyd Wright (Loren Pope and Jerry A. McCoy)

Above: In the familiar context of Wright's horizontal style, the Pope-Leighey House features natural cypress panels and cutout windows (Ping Amranand). Right: This preliminary drawing was produced in Wright's office in 1939 (Frank Lloyd Wright Foundation). Opposite: The interior of natural wood, beneath its clerestory crown, had upholstery, curtains, and carpeting all specified by Wright. Neutral rugs cover red concrete floors embedded with a radiant heating system (Ping Amranand)

On Jackson Place in Washington, Decatur House still surveyed Lafayette Park, now filled with statuary and surrounded by tall and formidable new government buildings. They had replaced all but a few of the row houses and mansions of what had been Washington's most elegant neighborhood for most of the nineteenth century. Corcoran's mansion was gone. Some of the old neighboring houses remained, of course: the White House, Dolley Madison's old house, occupied by the Cosmos Club, and St. John's Church and the great Second Empire mansion next door. Around the corner were other houses, notably Blair House. By the close of the 1920s an axe hung over all but the White House in the form of a law that called for the condemnation for government purposes of the real estate in the vicinity. The law was exercised piecemeal through the 1930s and accounted for the big federal office blocks.

Decatur House was occupied by the widow of Mary and Edward Beale's son, Truxtun. Marie Oge Beale first started to yield to the law, then, following Truxtun's death, she became committed to defying it. No one, least of all she, probably believed that there was a possibility of winning against the government. Decatur House was a special place to her, besides being her home. Old Washington kept house there now more than anywhere else. The Depression and the New Deal had changed the capital into a different sort of place. Some of Washington's best social events had always taken place at Decatur House, in the tradition begun by General and Mrs. Beale—notably the Washington reception for diplomats, which followed the annual winter diplomatic reception at the White House, and an open house after the president's New Year's Day reception. Although the White House no longer held this reception after 1933, the old guard still called that day at Decatur House, and the tall drawing rooms smelled of French perfume, ham, and whiskey, with an occasional whiff of mothballs.

Marie Beale kept society's lamp burning at Decatur House, not without difficulty at first. Memories of her beginning years here were not always pleasant. At the outset Washington had not received Marie Beale, as Truxtun's second wife, for people still resented Beale's divorce from his popular first wife, Harriet, daughter of Vice President James G. Blaine. It was a stormy divorce, ending an unhappy, often bitter marriage. Truxtun's early, stellar career in the Foreign Service abruptly ended after his father's death, when he rejected so confining a life. The wildfire his father had burned in himself during an adventurous youth and young manhood had been suppressed in the son, and he broke away from the imposed confinement to seek himself. He and Harriet and their son moved to Decatur House to join his mother, but he soon went on to California. In the divorce proceedings he fought hard to gain custody of the son, that the boy might grow up free of so stilted a life.

He lost and went away again; then came Marie and the scandal. The youthful Marie Oge had smitten a restless Beale when she was single, living in California. They stirred gossip. When a San Raphael newspaper editor in 1902 commented on Marie, Truxtun and a friend sought him out and beat

Marie Beale, seen with her Scotties about 1940, loved Decatur House and its history and determined that it would survive the onslaught of federal building in the neighborhood (Decatur House)

him to death. A furor ensued, and a hearing. Both were acquitted. After Truxtun and Marie married in 1903, they returned, oddly enough, to Decatur House. Mary Beale, his mother, was dead, and the house was empty. Henry Adams, a Lafayette Square neighbor, noted that "Truxtun's girl" was in town. Otherwise, the Beales were very visibly unnoticed. Harriet stepped forward from the silence of Washington. To break the ice, she hoped forever, and remove the volatile Truxtun from her and her son's lives, the former wife called on Marie. She found her "respectable and pretty; a kind of summer-girl." With years, Marie Beale won nearly everyone. In middle life she was tall and long necked, her hair neatly dressed in a stylish marcel; she knew how to talk and entertain. As she grew more certain of herself, much of her sense of place and well-being became tied up in the house on Lafayette Park.

Her opposition to condemnation efforts in the Depression years was constant. City officials dogged her continually about building codes—electricity, plumbing, and the rest. She maintained the house, but, like most old houses, Decatur House leaned a bit in parts and could have used a restoration. Marie Beale loved it and its buildup of ivory paint and layers and layers of things from all over the world, not the least her own collection of Latin American objects. On the drawing room table mixed with silver-framed photographs, bud vases, and books was William and Agnes Bourn's little volume, *Some Favorites.*

Marie Beale learned by heart the human history of her historic house, acquiring any artifacts and furnishings said to have been there. A partial restoration was made to the outside, to the two facades General Beale had modernized sixty years before; the brownstone trim was removed, and a fanlight was built in the doorway on the main front. An antiques dealer brought Marie Beale a set of drawings that proved to be Benjamin Henry Latrobe's original plans for the house. They were prominently displayed inside. When General Beale's fancy ceilings began to flake off, she had them painted anew, to preserve the Victorian character of the upstairs rooms.

Some encouragement came at the beginning of World War II, when F.D.R. personally halted the proposed demolition of Blair House so that it could be used to house overflow guests from the White House. Marie Beale realized that a precedent had been established for saving a house in this old neighborhood. But what about its preservation over years to come? The Cosmos Club, located in Dolley Madison's house, finally yielded to the government, and for a while it seemed that this landmark might go. It did not.

Marie Beale spent decades worrying and maneuvering over the survival of Decatur House. Within the brick walls, she and her guests felt the warmth of times gone by, as though some things never changed. One evening just after the war, at the height of a large dinner party, the floor of her library downstairs gave way, dumping guests all about. A few cuts and bruises later, the company gathered upstairs for nightcaps. The hostess had but one concern: the city inspector! Everyone was sworn to secrecy, and this pledge was kept faithfully until after Marie Beale was dead and Decatur House belonged to the National Trust.

Marie Beale had her library in the south rooms on the first floor of Decatur House, which today are refurnished as Stephen and Susan Decatur's dining and living rooms (Historic American Buildings Survey)

A Place for the Past

With the creation of any special place, there eventually comes to those who have kept it the question of its perpetuation beyond themselves. Weeks Hall was already confronting this question in the early 1930s, a decade after he completed restoring the Shadows. William Bourn was the exception, although the idea of what would happen to Filoli must have occurred to him in those hard fourteen years as an invalid. Realist that he was, he may have swept aside any notion of control beyond the grave. Not so the others, who saw in the beauty and history of their houses, as well as the heart they had given them, something that must be preserved. Where there was money to make this happen, success was relatively easy to imagine, but there was not always enough money.

A house may endure for generations, then, suddenly, is gone. Old houses survive as a rule because they remain useful. Fires and storms make occasional exceptions, and so can decay. But people have the power to stop decay. The houses in this book have been kept by successions of individuals who passed them on to others willing to

Opposite: The decorative work at Drayton Hall makes its interiors a remarkable colonial reflection of seventeenth- and eighteenth-century England. Even with its worn, ancient paint, this doorway, looking toward the main staircase, shows John Drayton's conscious effort to achieve magnificence in the design of his house. Rich pilasters cut from bald cypress are crowned by a cornice composed of egg-and-dart borders and, below, vertical triglyphs punctuated by stylized versions of lotuses and thistles carved in wood (Ping Amranand)

❧

Preceding pages: Montpelier, James Madison's home, looks out onto the Virginia countryside. "The range of mountains...extend as far as the eye can reach, forming successions of landscapes varied at every turn, from the wildest to the most cultivated...," observed Dolley Madison's niece Mary Cutts about 1817 (Robert Lautman)

hold on. Most of them suffered hard times, then were prosperous again. The natural process common to nearly all houses is cut short, it would appear, when they leave private hands and become properties of the National Trust for Historic Preservation. Today each of the houses here is a museum of its architecture and its history. For the most part, no one lives in them. Being drawn from real life, with all of its uncertainties, to a state of institutional preservation is a radical change. How did the houses in this book become properties of the National Trust?

By inheritance, Drayton Hall descended in part to Charlotta Drayton, one of three children of Charles Henry Drayton, the boy soldier. He died in 1915, at the age of sixty-eight, a man of substantial means. She was thirty and unmarried. Of all of the heirs, Charlotta took the greatest interest in the family history. Her father had always kept the house, if not generously, certainly in a state of preservation. Not a single pipe of plumbing pierced its walls, nor was electricity installed. Ancient paint covered the old paneling, worn so much in some places where the grain of the cypress showed through. At times in its history, Charlotta knew, wind and rain had blown on these fine walls, through hollow window sockets, until her father replaced the windows and put on the tin roof with the first money from the family's phosphate mining.

Thereafter, the ancestral home of the Draytons was never restored like other houses were restored. Through the 1930s and 1940s, when people in Charleston began consciously "restoring" their houses, bringing in older antiques to replace newer heirlooms, Drayton Hall stood unchanged, except for a continued rhythm of patching. During the 1930s Charlotta did venture to paint two rooms a bit brightly. She must have learned her lesson, for she painted no more.

She was a small woman and is remembered as being unassuming—"as becomes a lady," one of her friends emphasized—but she was not without opinions of her own. In her world she knew everyone, and her sister-in-law Emily's lack of interest in Drayton Hall gave Charlotta command over it, which she grasped and held tightly. It was generally understood in the family that the house was Aunt "Charley's" territory. Here she came for happy afternoons, whenever someone would come along to drive her, for she did not drive, and here her dogs ran free; she was very seldom apart from her accompaniment of canines, a numerous pack of mutts, each member with its name and beloved attributes, like General Beale's horses at Decatur House. Living a life as regular as a clock ticking, she imposed a rigid form on her allotment of time on earth. In spring, in the flowery peak of the season, she and several friends and all of the dogs moved to Drayton Hall, remaining several weeks until the heat and insects drove them away. Richmond Bowens, a descendant of plantation slaves and tenants who serves as a gatekeeper at Drayton Hall today, remembers how this chatelaine had for

Charles Henry Drayton of Drayton Hall stands with his family about 1910. From the left are his son Charles Drayton V, daughter Charlotta Drayton, wife Eliza Merritt Gantt Drayton, and daughter Eliza Gantt Drayton (Drayton Hall)

Noted photographer Frances Benjamin Johnston recorded the Draytons' Great Hall in the 1930s. Its eighteenth-century paneling remained, but the original ceiling had fallen and was replaced with another in the nineteenth century. On the wall is a painting of Mary Middleton Shoolbred Drayton, wife of Charles Drayton II, who may have installed the ceiling (Library of Congress)

her sole source of electricity extension cords run from the caretaker's house.

The rooms at Drayton Hall were sparsely furnished, with a few antiques and castoffs from home in Charleston, all assembled like the furnishings of a beach house. Pushed against the wall of one fine chamber, the weathered frame of old John Drayton's Chippendale-style serving table remained through good times and bad. Heaped up in the silent, cobwebbed basement were the parts of stone columns and carved architectural ornaments that had been left unused so long ago. Little else remained to show past habitation, except scars and wear on the house. In an upstairs room the pencilled height marks of a generation of children still could be discerned on a door frame. Many of the rooms were unused. Their worn, waxed floors and walls of wood and moist plaster were something beyond mellow, neglected not quite to the point of decay.

Charlotta Drayton brought together whatever family papers she could find and tediously transcribed them. Her work extended to six notebooks, mostly letters by twentieth-century Draytons. The later Draytons she had known personally in many instances. She recounted the Civil War tale of Uncle John saving the house with smallpox warnings, a story she had heard often from his own lips. Her interests placed her alongside others doing research in her remote community. The 1930s to the 1950s were productive years in understanding and recording the cultural history of Charleston. Some of the research centered on architecture, for the remarkable state of physical survival of the city was just being recognized. Architect Samuel Stoney made measured drawings of Drayton Hall, detailing its carved overmantels and rich plasterwork ceilings. Scholars Milby Burton and Anna Wells Rutledge studied furniture and silver. Charlotta's difference was that the past to her was only Drayton past—she the monastic scribe setting down the annals. When she was in her eighties, in the 1960s, the great question she asked herself was, Who would preserve Drayton Hall after her?

Bessie Chew, who was to be Aunt Bessie at Cliveden in later years, is seen here as a young woman with her brother Oswald about 1882 (Cliveden Archives)

ary Chew of Cliveden was Samuel's widow for forty years, beloved in Philadelphia for her kind heart and noble civic achievements. When she died in 1927, at the age of eighty-seven, she was survived by all but one of her six children. The second oldest, Bessie, had lived on unmarried with her and had adopted her parents' interest in the relics of the family. At sixty-four Bessie became the principal tenant of Cliveden and hostess to those who came to see it and hear its tales. Thin and proper Aunt Bessie, as the younger family called her, set up something of a throne room in the columned hallway, where she received dressed in black, poured tea, and conducted herself in ways perhaps a bit jollier and a tad more informal than had her staunch great aunt, Anne Sophia Penn Chew, whom she, of course, remembered well.

Through her thirty remaining years, Bessie "held court," as her nieces and nephews describe it. Financially secure, she was blessed with plenty of assistance in whatever she did. Kindly but not numerous servants filled her cup whenever it became empty; if a pesky city inspector called, he was likely not received. Germantown's continued growth as a suburb may have been a reminder that times had changed, but Cliveden still seemed quite apart from the town. More than that, it often appeared removed from the world; although Bessie and Cliveden outlived the Depression, two wars, the A Bomb, and Korea, and survived into the age of Elvis Presley, this detachment was as characteristic of her, particularly as her health declined, as of her house. Her nephew Sam had owned Cliveden since he was five years old. Did she wonder if he would love it as she had?

he National Trust for Historic Preservation was conceived two years after the close of World War II, in 1947, by leaders in existing historical groups and agencies, public and private, as a new, private organization that would use private funds to save and preserve a wide variety of historic sites. The term adopted was *historic preservation*. Even the word *preservation* labeled the movement as new. It was not the most compelling word to use for a battle cry; because *conservation* and *salvation* were already under venerable claim, eventually this placid word took on a life of its own, identifying it with keeping old buildings standing.

The eyes of the National Trust's founders had been opened to the nation's many historic places by the 1930s cultural programs of the New Deal. Surveys researched and recorded historic buildings, and the National Park Service accelerated efforts to restore historic sites for public education and enjoyment. The postwar development boom threatened America's historic landscape as surely as prewar poverty had helped it hold on. This patrimony of buildings was as valuable to the country as our famous natural wonders, but because such places lacked popular support and were always considered private (and thus not the concern of the public), they seemed destined to be obliterated by the advance of progress. It was clearer by 1947 that with the demise of the New Deal, federal money would no longer be available for saving historic sites, at least not without deadly delays in red tape and thus politics. Emergency, a byword of the 1930s, was passé in government in the 1940s. Historic preservation often involves emergencies, and it needed a friend in Washington.

The National Trust for Historic Preservation was chartered by Congress and signed into law by President Truman on October 26, 1949. "The purposes of the National Trust," explained the charter, "shall be to receive donations of sites, buildings, and objects significant in American history and culture, to preserve and administer them for public benefit." It was to be a truly national organization with a dues-paying membership; it was authorized to own properties, to engage in preservation campaigns to rescue buildings not its own, and to maintain educational programs. Through the years that followed, as the Trust grew, it questioned and refined its objectives, for it was itself the product of many disciplines, from architecture to archaeology to the antiquarians who, as the main donors, fired by their love of old houses and antique furnishings, then exerted the most influence. It was thus houses that the Trust acquired, rather than public buildings and battlefields. For all of the spoons that were in the soup, there was a constant, still somewhat unresolved intellectual struggle on the part of those not so specialized in their interests, to find a place for historic preservation in American society.

As the National Trust founders had anticipated, threats to historic structures appeared constantly. Most attention in those days was drawn to buildings that were sufficiently outstanding to be considered monuments. An embroil over Woodlawn erupted in 1948, when the 130-acre estate was purchased from Senator Underwood's widow by a Belgian religious order, the Immaculate Heart of Mary Mission Society, for use as an international headquarters. The news of the sale came as a surprise. Senator Underwood had been dead for twenty years, and for the past few years Bertha Underwood had rented Woodlawn and herself lay very ill in a Philadelphia nursing home, under the guardianship of her children. Within a month of the church's purchase, a local foundation was established under the banner "Save Woodlawn for the Nation!"

In reviewing the battle to recover Woodlawn from the Roman Catholic order, one sees plenty of smoke, but the fire is more elusive. If the accusation is true that religious prejudice played a part, no evidence is found in the records. The stacks of typed letters of support for a museum house, many from antiquarians who were inspired by the fact that Mount Vernon was saved, demanded that Nelly Custis's estate prevail intact and not as a feature of a campus crowded with newer buildings. The Woodlawn Public Foundation took the matter to court, arguing that while Woodlawn was a national treasure, the mission society would be unable to show the house to the public, thus precluding its public use. One has to admire the foundation's brashness. However, it did win a judgment. The foundation was allowed four months to come up with $170,000 to pay the Underwood family, which was $5,000 more than it had agreed to accept from the mission society. Four months were extended to five. On February 22, 1949, the foundation's lawyers informed the court that the money was in hand, raised by donations. On May 21, 1949, Woodlawn became the property of the foundation, five months before the National Trust charter was signed.

The new National Trust set up offices in Washington, which remains its headquarters city, in a row house on Lafayette Park, near Marie Beale's Decatur House (where the Trust's own offices later were located). At the time, the White House was being gutted in a drastic "restoration" that sent most of its historic interior to landfill. Elsewhere in the nation, the bulldozer had become La Guillotine, beginning what was to become, with time, a reign of terror over the remains of the past in American towns and cities. It was a good time to start a National Trust. Eager to try its hand at preservation, the Trust in 1951 took a fifty-year lease on Woodlawn from the Woodlawn Foundation. The Trust's obligations in this lease were many, but Woodlawn proved a valuable showcase for the organization, and six years later it came under full ownership of the National Trust.

Edith Wilson moved with her husband to their S Street town house in Washington in 1921. After his death in 1924 she remained for the balance of her long life (Parade *Magazine, courtesy Woodrow Wilson House*)

Woodlawn, however, was not the first property owned by the National Trust. In 1953 notification came by telegram from California that Casa Amesti had been willed to the organization by Frances Adler Elkins. There was no endowment, for she left little money at all, just the house and its numerous contents, with the interiors about the same as they had been when she completed them more than thirty years before. The initial reaction might have been to reject the bequest for lack of funds to honor it, but, as the Trust was to learn in years to come, versatility was often the key to historic preservation, and success often appeared in strange costume. A way was found in Monterey. Casa Amesti was leased to a private eating club, the Old Capital Club, which today guards and preserves Frances Elkins's romantic melding of old California and the world as though she still lived there.

The Lafayette Park neighbor, Marie Beale, made it known in 1953 that through her new will the National Trust would inherit Decatur House and everything in it. She had no children. Truxtun's son by Harriet had died in World War I. Marie Beale had fought the good fight to save these old walls, and she would pass the battle flag to the Trust but remain there as long as she lived. Decatur House became a National Trust property in 1956.

In 1954 another Washington widow, Edith Wilson, informed the National Trust of her similar decision. Three of her ten years of marriage to

214

Woodrow Wilson had been spent in the red brick Embassy Row house. Here she had remained for thirty years, with her mementoes, the best clothes she had worn as First Lady, silver, china, diplomatic gifts, books. All of it went to the Trust intact seven years later, in 1961.

In Louisiana in the 1950s Weeks Hall's obsession to secure the future of the Shadows made a Gothic tale. As early as 1940 he had hoped to make an arrangement with the National Park Service to take his house when he died, maintaining it as a historic site. During the 1930s one of those New Deal programs, the Historic American Buildings Survey, made special note of the authenticity of the Shadows, and Weeks Hall believed that this gave him an advantage with the government. He wrote page after page of information about the property and how little he had done to change it. These notes he sent on to Washington, but World War II intervened. Official interest was not shown again.

Tourists wandered through his garden, and now and then he opened the house. It infuriated him that people wanted to see the inside of the house more than the exterior and the garden, which he considered the glory of the place. In his isolation he became ever more withdrawn into the Shadows, playing tricks on visitors—notably by wearing a mask and looking down from an attic window—and, on a social level, driving away with glares those

Outside a newly restored Shadows, Weeks Hall pauses in 1923 with the movie director D. W. Griffith, who was scouting film locations in Cajun country (courtesy Shadows-on-the-Teche)

he knew who did not interest him. He spent time with his camera, always with the Shadows as his subject. Although he had hurt one hand in an automobile accident, he may still have painted pictures, and one wonders if those that survived him with the weird colors and mildly pornographic subjects date from these years. As for money, his financial resources, which had only barely survived the 1920s, were less than ever.

The plantings around the Shadows grew thick, the camellias tall, and the aura of the garden became as detached from the world as its owner. Even the goldfish in the pond gained an old and gnarled, rather literary, appearance, and the numbers increased to crowd the water. In the mid-1950s Hall became desperate about the house. Perhaps it was some long-standing fear within him, or perhaps it was simply that a sudden, practical note in his lifelong symphony of impracticality told Weeks Hall that only he could work to save the Shadows from destruction, use as a funeral parlor, or purchase by some doctor's wife.

He repeated his story to anyone who would listen. Magazines, newspapers, radio, and national television publicized his plight. What a strange turnaround it was for one who had so rejected the world to fall on his knees before it, begging it to save the only thing he had ever loved. Friends realized that his health was failing. He sent letter upon letter to historical organizations, and finally he caught the eye of the National Trust, of which he knew nothing, only that it would listen. Told he needed to put up an endowment that would help maintain the property, he called his lawyer and made an accounting of what he had: a figure, sum total, of about $170,000—not high, but not so low in the mid-1950s.

The money must be kept intact, to save the house. He fed no guests anymore, and he practically lived on peanut butter, spending as little as possible on himself. "Will they take my house?" he asked again and again. Drawing near the end of his days, he discouraged the visit of a close friend, Sarah Helm, from across the bayou. "Don't worry about me, Sarah," he laughed over the telephone, "I'm not going to die until I know if they'll take my house. You can count on that." The Trust returned with a positive answer in June 1958, and he died only days later.

Belle Grove was accepted by the National Trust in 1964, an endowed bequest by its botanist-restorer, Francis Welles Hunnewell. Lyndhurst came to the Trust in the same year, willed by the aged Anna Gould, who died in France. Belle Grove was the secluded retreat of a scholar and served its quiet purpose for nearly forty years. Lyndhurst provides a more varied history. For many years it was kept and cherished by the eldest Gould daughter, Helen, who had purchased it from her father's estate. The mansion became a shrine to her parents. Furnishings were left as they had used them. Helen allowed no one but herself to sleep in their great Gothic bed, in the vaulted room over the front parlor. Just when it seemed that the prim, tweedy Miss Gould

Above left: Anna Gould, then Countess Castellane, and her first husband, Count Paul-Ernest Boniface de Castellane, take a ride in their Panhard electric car about 1900. Above right: Helen Gould Shepard greets guests with her children about 1914 (both, Lyndhurst)

would remain single all of her life, she married at forty-four a Gould employee, Finley J. Shepard, a dapper and charming man with whom she was very happy. For the children she and Shepard adopted, she created at Lyndhurst pleasures matching those of her own childhood, all the while carrying out her own quiet philanthropies.

When Helen Gould Shepard died in 1938, Finley Shepard had no wish to keep the estate or have its costs deprive his and Helen's children of what they might inherit. At this point it could have been lost, had its plight not alarmed the younger sister, Anna, who had lived most of her life in France. Remembering happy years at home, she purchased Lyndhurst in 1939 to save it, and when she returned there and walked through its rooms alone she relived her girlhood. Soon she took an apartment at the Plaza Hotel in New York and spent much of her time there and at Lyndhurst.

She was the Duchesse de Talleyrand-Perigord, widowed at about the time Helen died. As a young woman she had broken an engagement to an American businessman to marry Count Boniface de Castellane and move to France. This union ended in divorce, but the second marriage to Helie, Duc de Talleyrand-Perigord, succeeded. Her life, however, had been miserable. Three of her four sons died young, and the fourth committed suicide over his parents' refusal to permit his marriage to a woman of whom they did not approve. Anna Gould was a restless woman in later years, long resident in France, but never "French" like her husband and children. She often longed for home and envied her sister's happiness. Lyndhurst recalled to her old, brief days of peace, and she tucked herself away when there in the tower bedroom she had used in her childhood and was content.

She worried for years over what would happen to Lyndhurst when she died. In 1957 she made a will leaving the estate to the village of Tarrytown.

"My father loved it," she wrote of Lyndhurst in the will, "as did my sister, and as I do. We loved its broad acres, its stately trees, its unsurpassed view, and particularly the atmosphere of peace, of quiet, and of contentment which prevails. . . . The days of my childhood spent there, I count among the happiest of my life." Two years later, in 1959, she changed her will, leaving Lyndhurst to the National Trust. In 1961, old and tired, she returned to her daughter in France, never to come back to America. She changed her will over and over before her death later that year.

The National Trust emerged from a three-year legal battle to take possession of Lyndhurst at last in 1964. Opposition to the preservation of the estate and its 550 acres had come from many fronts, from the heirs in Paris, from local real estate development interests, and, less convincingly, from some who opposed a memorial to a "robber baron." But, after all, it was the Gould tenure that was the most authentically preserved at Lyndhurst and ultimately the most significant episode in the history of the house. Defeated at about the same time in very public efforts to save a Gothic house in Connecticut, the Harral-Wheeler Mansion in Norwalk, designed by Lyndhurst's architect, A. J. Davis, the Trust was fit for battle, and it won this one.

During the Lyndhurst negotiations, a drama took place that was to be far more significant to the historic preservation movement: the effort to preserve the 1941 house designed by Frank Lloyd Wright for the Pope family, known today as the Pope-Leighey House. Loren and Charlotte Pope lived in their Usonian house throughout the war, but it became too cramped to remain there longer. They purchased a farm, and Wright, happy to retain so willing a client, came to select a site for the new house he had agreed to design for them. This second Pope house was never built. Meanwhile, in 1946, the Popes sold the house in Falls Church, Virginia, to Marjorie and Robert Leighey, a couple with no children who were in search of a special house in which to live. Toward the close of the 1950s, Robert Leighey's poor health kept the Leigheys fairly confined to home, and their busy lives and sentiments became much centered in this house. They entertained in it, worked there every day, and obligingly showed curious scholars through the house by appointment. When they received notice in 1961 that a highway, Interstate 66, was to be built through the property, their reaction can be imagined. A few months later, two rows of wooden stakes were driven through their property, with the house standing in between. Marjorie Leighey protested but was largely ignored by state officials, so she went to the press. A small flutter rose but soon subsided.

Robert Leighey died in the summer of 1963, and in October "Marjorie F. Leighey, widow," received a demand from state officials that she sign their option to purchase her house. Small, dark-haired Marjorie Leighey was not one to be pushed around, and she became even less so as the arrogance of Virginia officials increasingly offended her. She consulted her lawyer, and they decided to ignore the state's correspondence. But by the winter of the next year, Marjorie Leighey knew that there was little hope in a lone stand and turned to the U.S. Department of the Interior and, soon after that, the National Trust. It was clear that accommodation would have been made by the state had the house been colonial instead of a suburban, ranch-style house not thirty years old. A compromise was finally reached: move the house to a site in the forest at Woodlawn in nearby Mount Vernon, Virginia. It was the least desirable solution, but it would preserve the house.

Marjorie Leighey donated her piece of Usonia and the condemnation money to the National Trust, retaining for herself a life estate to live in the house if she desired. The Pope-Leighey House—or rather, the wooden and metal parts of the house—was moved between the fall of 1964 and the summer of 1965 and the building reassembled. It occupies a forest site elevated on the back side above the roadway to the house at Woodlawn, and on the front it nestles at the foot of a long slope. Marjorie Leighey, off on a missionary assignment, did return to the house four years later and remained until her death in 1983.

She looked on her house as even more special than before, preserving everything about it, even to stuffing worn towels and nylon hosiery into the chairs Wright had designed, so that the sprung cushions would keep their shape. On Sunday tours she lectured to paying visitors about life in the house in its two locations, and she still recoiled in anger at the mention of the gleaming concrete river that was becoming Interstate 66. When a visitor congratulated her on having her house saved, she replied, "It has nothing to do with me whatsoever. My house was saved because it was designed by Frank Lloyd Wright."

After saving her house, Marjorie Leighey posed on its new site at Woodlawn in 1967 (courtesy Frank Lloyd Wright's Pope-Leighey House and Jerry A. McCoy)

Oatlands became a National Trust property in 1965, the first outright donation, with an endowment, that was not a bequest in a will. It was given in memory of Billy and Edith Eustis by their daughters, Anne Emmet and Margaret Finley. Both women sincerely regretted permitting the demolition of the Corcoran mansion in Washington many years before, and they hoped to assure that Oatlands escaped the same fate. David Finley, Margaret's husband and one of the Trust's founders, was a good one to advise them. Long a leading figure in arts and historical organizations, he had been director of the National Gallery of Art. He doubted that the history of the house would mean much, in the absence of the early Carter furnishings, but he thought that people might simply admire it as a beautiful house. He replaced many furnishings, quite certain that "the public will want to see better things than were here." Oatlands was made into a museum house, reflecting the Eustis years from the turn of the century until after World War II. It has remained active as a center for horse sports.

Margaret French Cresson had used Chesterwood as her summer home since the loss of her husband and parents in the 1930s. A prize-winning sculptor, she realized more and more the importance of her father's work and the American Renaissance in art and architecture of which he was so intimate a part. Personable as ever, she was for long years a winter resident in Washington, D.C., and New York, where many of her old friends lived, but she moved back at last to Stockbridge, spending the worst part of winters in Florida. After her, there would be no family member to keep Chesterwood. It would have to be sold or given away. She alone was there to make the sacrifice.

For some years she tried different approaches. In summers in the 1950s she opened French's studio to the public. Sometimes she gave tours herself, pointing out the plaster of the great seated *Lincoln*, but keeping a cloth covering over the marble figure *Andromeda*, her father's last work, which stayed exactly where he had left it. Virtually no changes had been made to the studio; here still were French's tools and sketches, his collections of statues and books all around. Bottled chemicals, soap, and brushes lined the shelves in the casting room. Although she considered other organizations, in 1969, in her eightieth year, Margaret French Cresson donated Chesterwood to the National Trust. She died four years later in the house her parents had built.

Painter John C. Johansen, a friend of the French family, portrayed Margaret and William Penn Cresson at home in 1921, the first summer of their marriage. Their cottage near Chesterwood, the Dormouse, was a wedding gift from Margaret's father (Paul Rocheleau, Chesterwood Collection)

Bessie Chew lived a longer life than both Margaret Cresson and her mother, Mary Chew. Born at Cliveden in 1863, during the Civil War, she died a resident of the same house in 1958, at the age of ninety-five. She had never owned Cliveden, yet it was as much hers as it had been Anne Sophia's. Every Sunday she served ice cream to her nieces and nephews. These children of modern times entered the dark house as one might enter a tomb—"screaming Sundays," they called the ice cream sessions—but they faithfully attended. Aunt Bessie sat, thin as a pencil, banked against cushions on the settee in the hall, and dished up the treats. The house was tatty. Once, in an attempt to save appearances, a niece hung some discarded damask draperies in the parlor and used the extras to reupholster the old armchairs. In her last years, Bessie was blind. Company still delighted her, and she was unabashed in asking a visitor to read to her from a new book or even an old favorite. She knew her house, from the shattered battle doors against the wall to the smallest sewing basket. A relative looking for something was directed upstairs to a certain bedroom, to a certain bureau, where, on the left side of the third drawer down, the object would be found, and it was.

When her journey ended at last, Cliveden went, physically and spiritually, to the male heir who had owned the house since his Uncle Samuel died in 1919, childless and unmarried. Samuel Chew III had been only a young boy when he fell heir to the house. His Uncle Sam had suggested in the year he died that some organization be given Cliveden, for it was too much for the family to keep. Yet he passed it on. By 1958 the house had a generous mixture of furniture from many generations. Young Sam wanted the house to look right. He began a program of weeding out furnishings not appropriate to the earliest years of the house. Items not sold or given away were moved to the barn to share quarters with the old Chew coach and the battle doors that had stood for so long in the entrance hall.

Inside, the house was edited to a look of period perfection, more readily associated with assemblages of antiques-shop merchandise than the mix of things in a family home. The look, an interior decorator sort of concept, received art status in the 1920s in the American Wing of the Metropolitan Museum of Art and by the 1950s was admired even still, somewhat updated, in the dressy rooms of Winterthur, the residence and museum of Henry Francis du Pont near Wilmington, Delaware. Connoisseurs had admired Cliveden's chests and sofa and fine eighteenth-century mirrors for years, while scorning the "later" things that shared the rooms with them. Du Pont himself helped Sam Chew with the corrections at Cliveden. Suddenly it was a different house.

Tight personal finances and Cliveden's many demands weighed heavily on Chew after a time. Germantown's disadvantages presented themselves in security fears. This house was not a burden one could simply abandon, and Chew was the first to admit it. He began talking to the National Trust, which was naturally interested in the idea of bringing under its protection so major a site in American history. In 1970 arsonists set fire to the barn. The battle doors that had withstood Washington's assault in 1777 were lost, as were all

Samuel Chew, the last private owner of Cliveden, stands on the front lawn beside a battle-scarred statue about 1960 (Cliveden Archives)

but fragments of the historic Chew coach and what was left of the furniture taken out when the house was redecorated. Financial arrangements were completed, and in 1972 Cliveden joined the houses of the National Trust.

In the same year, the estate of Frances Mary Molera was settled, leaving the adobe house of her grandfather, John Cooper, to the National Trust. She had died four years before at the age of eighty-nine, unmarried, in the genteel confines of her quiet life in San Francisco, a patron of her church, historical study, and one of her state's most generous donors to the cause of preserving open land. She had long protected John Cooper's house in Monterey, across the street from its sister, Casa Amesti. Separated into two houses in 1833 because her grandfather needed money, the property was returned to Cooper family ownership in 1900, when Cooper's older daughter purchased it; the two parcels went to Frances Mary Molera on the deaths of her mother and aunt. Through a cooperative agreement between the Trust and the state of California, more than a decade of research, archaeology, and restoration was begun, resulting in a museum complex of old Monterey called the Cooper-Molera Adobe.

The death of Charlotta Drayton at eighty-four in 1968 passed Drayton Hall on to her nephews. Aunt Charley expressed in her will her hope that one of them might preserve it, but neither was able to do so. They loved the place. It was heart and soul, and a white elephant, but it was also a valuable asset. The dilemma kept the nephews from making an immediate decision, as real estate agents hovered. At last the 650-acre property, highly desirable for industrial development, was put on the market to the highest bidder. Preservationists in Charleston joined efforts with the state of South Carolina, the Historic Charleston Foundation, and the National Trust, with the cooperation of Aunt Charley's nephews. The house, held under lease for a short time, became a Trust property in 1974, for a relatively low price of about a thousand dollars an acre, including the house and all of its historic subsidiary buildings. After debate on the subject, the Trust decided not to restore Drayton Hall, but to keep it patched, as the Draytons had done for more than a century.

A portrait of Lurline Roth by Lloyd Sexton in a drawing room at Filoli shows her in her gardening clothes, holding one of her favorite flowers, a rose (John Vaughan)

Just in advance of the national bicentennial celebration, three more properties came into the National Trust. Frank Lloyd Wright's Oak Park complex was nearly forgotten until his death in 1959 renewed interest in his early career. The home and studio was purchased by a foundation created for the purpose in 1974. Wright's studio had been the most changed, in part by Wright himself. Early in the 1950s the owner asked him to do work on the house. Wright, then into his eighties, came to Oak Park, but not for long. Personal memories overtook him, and he left, never to return. The house was a mirror of a private past, long set aside, reflecting his formative and, to Wright, innocent years.

Ownership of the property was transferred to the National Trust in 1975, with the restoration and management of the house museum retained by the Frank Lloyd Wright Home and Studio Foundation. The building has been restored to its appearance in 1909, Wright's last year in the house.

Lurline Roth, a widow for many years, donated Filoli and its garden in 1975, with a lease on eighty-six acres more; seven years later the balance of 529 acres was joined to the gift and an endowment provided $2.5 million.

Brucemore in Iowa had fared better financially than any house in these pages. In comparison to them, it existed on a silk pillow, always maintained and groomed, its large grounds cared for lovingly—no weeds, no leaks; in short, no poverty, and very watchful eyes. After the widow Caroline Sinclair traded the Queen Anne mansion to George Bruce Douglas of Quaker Oats and his wife, Irene, the estate became almost a portrait of Irene Douglas. In her many years there, she expanded the gardens and continually remodeled parts of the house. Margaret, the eldest of three daughters, inherited Brucemore when her widowed mother died in 1937. To an extent the house, although Margaret's, was always to remain Irene's.

Margaret Hall was the wife of Howard Hall, a businessman of great skill whose interests burgeoned over a relatively few years into steel and heavy construction equipment, presidency of the Amana Refrigeration Company of the Amana colonies in Iowa, and eventually into banking. The Halls had no children. Their private lives were not those one usually associates with preoccupied business executives. They were together nearly all of the time, living among several houses, but they were happiest when at home. Hospitality was frequent and lively at Brucemore. To amuse their guests, they built a basement retreat called the Grizzly Bar and, nearby, the

Above: Margaret Douglas Hall inherited Brucemore from her mother in 1937. Left: Howard Hall, Margaret's husband, kept a pet lion there (both, Brucemore Archives)

sensual Tahitian room, which was piped to shed "rain" on its tin roof, recalling Maugham's Pacific. Brucemore included luxurious accommodations for a lion, among numerous pets of Howard Hall.

The house was kept up-to-date. Cream-colored paint covered the dark Queen Anne woodwork, and lace curtains were replaced by tailored linen. Flower gardening was an interest of Margaret Hall, and she employed a staff of gardeners. Bouquets from her cutting gardens were sent out practically every day, whether she knew the recipients or simply admired them from afar for some reason. Margaret is remembered as quiet and gentle, always in contrast to her husband, and the two of them demanded good times from life.

Assuring Brucemore's well-being was a simple matter for Margaret Hall. She wanted the estate preserved, perhaps more because of her mother than for her own memories. When the issue presented itself, on Howard's death in 1971, she considered various options. In 1976 she presented the house to the National Trust, with a provision that she remain there the balance of her life. The donation of Brucemore was only one of Margaret Hall's charities, but she wanted the house to be enjoyed by her community as more than a museum. National Trust officials remember the day the lawyers telephoned from Cedar Rapids in 1981 to say that the property now belonged to the Trust. No one in the office recalled the arrangement about Brucemore until reminded by forgotten files. Margaret Hall had made her gift and not contacted the Trust again. Its endowment, increased over the years, is the highest of any National Trust property.

Marion du Pont Scott enjoyed equestrian events at Montpelier and elsewhere (Raymond Woolfe Collection)

If the acquisition of Brucemore came as a surprise, then the inheritance of Montpelier two years later, in 1983, was a shock. Marion du Pont Scott, months before her ninetieth birthday, had changed her will in secret with her lawyer, leaving Montpelier to the National Trust. No prior negotiations of any kind, or even conversations, had been carried on with the Trust. It was Marion Scott's style. Alas, as it turned out, the home of James Madison was not hers to give, because by her father's will it was to go, after her death, to the children of her brother, Willie. The Trust elected to pursue the matter. A settlement eventually was reached. Nearly all of the furnishings were removed from the house by the du Pont heirs, and they accepted cash settlements from money left with the house and farm.

After a year, in 1984, the estate of some 2,400 acres and the house became the property of the National Trust, including the store, railroad station, racetrack, and more than a hundred farm buildings, from tenant houses to ready-cut Sears, Roebuck barns. Three years later the empty house, open to the public, was central to a debate over whether it should be left as William du Pont had remodeled it nearly a century before, or whether modern technical skills should be brought to bear in restoring the much-altered building to its appearance when it was the home of James and Dolley Madison. The case does not yet rest.

These seventeen houses, protected today and open to the public, are not always frozen as their last occupants left them. Their own long histories have shown that to be impossible. They are subject to change through historical interpretation; by the illustrations in this book, one can see that in some cases the houses have been restored to represent earlier periods in their history. Most of the houses are kept flexible and used for many purposes, as well as museums. About half of the properties are managed directly by the National Trust, and the rest are in a status known as costewardship, where management is in the hands of a local organization that works in cooperation with the Trust. Additional houses are in the process of acquisition—notably the Glass House in Connecticut built by architect Philip Johnson and Kykuit, John D. Rockefeller's Hudson River estate near Lyndhurst—or are being brought under protective easements in which the Trust will legally control any future changes and uses that might affect the architecture or setting of the property. The Trust's headquarters in Washington at 1785 Massachusetts Avenue is an early twentieth-century French-style *hôtel,* one of the city's finest Beaux Arts mansions and variously the Washington address of such notables as Andrew Mellon.

To preserve is to keep. As the meaning of preservation in the United States has been stretched and revised, the houses of the National Trust have been seen more clearly as representative of a movement. They speak in many tongues. One can, of course, hear them for what they say about their own architecture, craftsmanship, and fine materials, or their settings; one can review the personalities—the tenants—who have passed through them and kept them. These are usual pursuits followed by people who like old houses, but few old houses are available to be enjoyed in this way by the public.

Today there is more. Even beyond history and nostalgia, the houses play a distinct role in American life because they are there. They are time that one can see and even touch, time then, time now, and a unique time future as well. Time forms a major theme, perhaps the dominant theme, in crowded, modern humankind living today in a world alongside technology. Time is abstract unless tagged, and buildings mark time in a language clearer in everyday life than even the written word. Their preservation gives shelter to some, but continuity and place to all.

Were the characters who kept the National Trust's houses concerned with this value? In a way, yes. If not perhaps in the broad sense in which we see it, they were aware that the houses provided a continuity of past and present in their own lives, and they saw that this was understood by other people—even people they did not know, visitors who came to look and enjoy. They believed that there was something worthwhile in continuing what had existed for so long, and they were willing to have their private domains become public. But most of all, they saw what they had as places of great beauty. This was reason enough that the houses must always remain.

Source Notes and Further Reading

The histories of the houses that have become National Trust properties can be reconstructed only by consulting a variety of sources. Some primary materials are kept at the houses themselves; the balance are in archives and libraries or in private hands. Of special value at the properties have been structural and archaeological reports, as well as specialized studies available only in manuscript form. Original and published manuscripts have been relied on wherever possible; the best published accounts have been consulted on special subjects. Some of these, as well as general and contextual works, may be of interest to the reader who wishes to probe deeper.

Colonial Empires

The best survey of the early colonial history of the South, the world that gave birth to Drayton Hall, is found in Wesley Frank Craven's *The Southern Colonies in the Seventeenth Century* (Baton Rouge, 1949 and 1970), the first volume of the Louisiana State University Press series A History of the South. George C. Rogers, *Charleston in the Age of the Pinckneys* (Norman, Okla., 1969), paints a vivid picture of life and living in the leading city of those colonies, and Samuel G. Stoney's *Plantations of the Carolina Low Country* (Charleston, 1938 and 1964) portrays the architecture of the region.

The vast Chew family papers are housed at the Historical Society of Pennsylvania and were consulted for the periods of Cliveden covered here. Burton Alva Konkle, *Benjamin Chew* (Philadelphia, 1932), is the only biography of the man who built the house. George B. Tatum, *Penn's Great Town* (Philadelphia, 1961), provides useful architectural context for it; Jennifer Anderson-Lawrence's unpublished master's thesis, "The Colonial Revival at Cliveden" (University of Delaware, 1990), is an interesting treatment of the later years.

Children of the Revolution

The plantation world of the upper South, in which the Madisons and Hites flourished, is the subject of Daniel Blake Smith's study *Inside the Great House* (Ithaca, N.Y., 1980). Charles S. Sydnor's *Gentlemen Freeholders* (Chapel Hill, 1952 and 1965), explores the political culture of pre-Revolutionary Virginia that produced the Father of the Constitution. Robert A. Rutland's *James Madison* (New York, 1987) is an excellent recent one-volume life. Conover Hunt-Jones's *Dolley and the "Great Little Madison"* (Washington, 1977) offers the best account of life at Montpelier. The definitive edition of Madison's *Papers* is being published by the University Press of Virginia, 16 vols. (Chicago and Charlottesville, 1962–), currently under the editorship of J. C. A. Stagg. The unpublished report on the architectural investigations of the much-altered Montpelier (1988) by Paul E. Buchanan, Charles A. Phillips, and Joseph K. Oppermann was most useful in recreating the house as the Madisons had it. Updates on architecutral research have been provided by Ann Miller and Larry Dermody at the site.

In addition to Civil War–era references described under Houses Divided, good sources on Belle Grove are A. C. Clark, ed., *Life and Letters of Dolley Madison* (Washington, 1914), and Samuel Kercheval, *A History of the Valley of Virginia* (Strasburg, Va., 1925). Thomas W. Dolan made available to me his historical studies and architectural analysis of Belle Grove. *Belle Grove* (Washington, 1968) was published by the National Trust as part of a small series of general overviews of its properties.

William W. Freehling's *The Road to Disunion* (New York, 1990) provides a good up-to-date scholarly treatment of the political and social history of the South between the Revolution and the Civil War; consult his endnotes for references to recent special studies. Eugene J. Genovese, *Roll, Jordan, Roll: The World the Slaves Made* (New York, 1974), examines life in the great houses from the perspective of the large supporting cast on whose labor the plantation system depended. *Within the Plantation Household* (Chapel Hill, 1988) by Elizabeth Fox-Genovese focuses on black and white women in the old South. Peter H. Wood, *Black Majority* (New York, 1974), deals with slavery in South Carolina from the mid-seventeenth to the mid-eighteenth century.

A number of Nelly Custis's letters have been published in *George Washington's Beautiful Nelly* (New Orleans, 1991), Patricia Brady, ed.; letters of her cousin in marriage, Rosalie Stier Calvert, appear in *Mistress of Riversdale* (Baltimore, 1991), Margaret Law Calcott, ed.; and Margaret Bayard Smith's letters and reminiscences recreate *The First Forty Years of Washington Society* (New York, 1906 and 1965), Gaillard Hunt, ed.

The Carters of Oatlands are chronicled in Barbara Dombrowski, *A History of Oatlands* (Leesburg, Va., n.d.), and the Carter family in Clifford Dowdey, *The Virginia Dynasties* (Boston, 1969), and his "The Age of 'King' Carter," *Iron Worker*, Spring 1968. See also Louis Morton, *Robert Carter of Nomini Hall* (Williamsburg, 1945). Some of my material on the twentieth century at Oatlands came from various conversations on the site in 1974 with David and Margaret Eustis Finley.

Susan and Stephen Decatur had important roles in the early history of Washington and appear in nearly all of the journals and memoirs of the time, but as yet there is no definitive book about them and the house they commissioned from Benjamin H. Latrobe. An extraordinary sequence of architectural drawings that have survived, as well as a collection of Decatur

House papers (such as the Beale family papers, pertaining principally to that family), are now in the Library of Congress. *The Correspondence and Miscellaneous Papers of Benjamin Henry Latrobe*, 3 vols. (New Haven, 1984–1988), publishes the important letters the architect wrote to his clients; Talbot Hamlin's biography, *Benjamin Henry Latrobe* (New York, 1955), is still useful on his career. Marie Beale's informal account of *Decatur House and Its Inhabitants* (Washington, 1954) captures the romance the house held for her. John Niven, *Martin Van Buren* (New York, 1983), is the best life of that brief but significant tenant of Decatur House; George W. Pierson's *Tocqueville and Beaumont in America* (New York, 1938) documents the famous French travelers' visit to Washington during Edward Livingston's residence. Judah P. Benjamin has been the subject of many books, not the least Vina Delmar's novel *Beloved* (New York, 1956). A recent biography is Eli N. Evans, *Judah P. Benjamin: The Jewish Confederate* (New York, 1988). Edward Fitzgerald Beale is the subject of Carl Briggs, *Quarterdeck and Saddlehorn* (Glendale, Calif., 1983), and Gerald Thompson, *Edward F. Beale and the American West* (Albuquerque, 1983); his exploits deserve more. Gossip of General Beale's day and that of his son, Truxtun, can be found in J. C. Levenson, Ernest Samuels, et al., eds., *The Letters of Henry Adams*, 6 vols. (Cambridge, Mass., 1982–1988). An overview of the house and its occupants was published by the National Trust as *Decatur House* (Washington, 1967).

Age of Enterprise

Cavalier and Yankee: The Old South and American National Character by William R. Taylor (New York, 1961) nicely revives the ethos of the antebellum South that gave birth to the Shadows and other mansions southerners built in the years before the Civil War. The Weeks papers are a large collection at the archives of Louisiana State University at Baton Rouge and take the scholar through all of the years, including the time of Weeks Hall. Romantic Louisiana, as seen in its architecture and landscape, can be visited in Lyle Saxon's classic *Old Louisiana* (New Orleans, 1929 and 1950) and Harnett T. Kane's *Plantation Parade* (New York, 1945). George W. Cable's *Strange, True Stories of Louisiana* (New York, 1889) delighted the Gilded Age with its descriptions of the bayous in old times. The best available account of Weeks Hall's garden is by Jamie Credle, "The Landscape of the Shadows-on-the-Teche," *Nineteenth Century* 10 (1991) 4: 7–11.

The architecture of Lyndhurst is described in many books, but by far the most thoughtful analysis is found in William H. Pierson, Jr., *American Buildings and Their Architects: Technology and the Picturesque, the Corporate, and the Early Gothic Styles* (Garden City, N.Y., 1978); Billie Sherrill Blitz, *The Greenhouse at Lyndhurst* (Washington, 1977), serves as a useful supplement. Those interested in the Pauldings, Washington Irving, and their circle will find relatively few published sources, but General Paulding's poet brother, James Kirke Paulding, left fine letters; see Ralph M. Aderman, ed., *Letters of James K. Paulding* (Madison, Wis., 1962). A. J. Davis's letters and drawings are in the New York Public Library and the Avery Architectural Library at

Columbia University; the architect's *Rural Residences* (New York, 1837, etc., and 1980) had wide influence in the nineteenth century. On the complex subject of the Goulds, Frank Kittrea's "The Realms of Gould," *American Heritage*, April 1970, is an interesting, swift account; Edwin Palmer Hoyt, *The Goulds* (New York, 1969), and Alice Northrop Snow and Henry Nicholas Snow, *The Story of Helen Gould* (New York, 1943), focus on family life and personalities. Maury Klein has written a comprehensive scholarly reevaluation of the great industrialist in *The Life and Legend of Jay Gould* (Baltimore, 1986). The needed scholarly reassessment of the post–Civil War era, called for by H. Wayne Morgan in his introduction to *The Gilded Age: A Reappraisal* (Syracuse, 1963, 1970), still has far to go.

The two adobes in Monterey are not as well documented as one might wish, but enough has turned up to paint their early portraits. California's romantic Mexican period was first given serious historical treatment by Hubert Howe Bancroft in his *History of California* (San Francisco, 1884–1890), vols. 13–19 of his *History of the Pacific States.* General Vallejo worked for many years producing a five-volume history of California, which remains in manuscript form, written with the express purpose of showing the Hispanic point of view. With considerable effort Bancroft gained the confidence of a suspicious Vallejo. The remarkable Vallejo Documentos are now held in the Bancroft Library, University of California, Berkeley. Myrtle M. McKittrick, *Vallejo: Son of California* (Portland, Ore., 1944) tells the general's story and that of some of his kin, but the subject cries out for a new interpretation. John Woolfendun and Amelie Elkinton, *Cooper: Juan Bautista Rogers Cooper, 1791–1872* (Pacific Grove, Calif., 1983), is based on rich documentation not only in manuscripts but in artifacts of the Cooper adobe. *California's Architectural Frontier* by Harold Kirker (San Marino, Calif., 1960) contains a good account of these houses. Another important resource for the Mexican and transitional periods is George Peter Hammond, et al., eds., *The Larkin Papers*, 11 vols. (Berkeley, Calif., 1951–1968). Dora P. Crouch, Daniel J. Garr, and Axel I. Mundigo, *Spanish City Planning in North America* (Cambridge, Mass., 1982), provides a larger context for the construction of the adobes.

Houses Divided

The basic resource for American history during the Civil War is *The War of the Rebellion: A Compilation of the Official Records of the Union and Confederate Armies*, 128 vols. (Washington, 1880–1901), available in nearly all large libraries. The unedited documents together with the records of the Freedmen's Bureau are today in the military record group of the National Archives. Although sources for the study of the Civil War are extensive, those for the particular houses and characters treated here are disappointingly slim—an exception being Belle Grove, which is richly documented in period newspapers, books, and letters. Notable among these is artist James E. Taylor's sketchbook and diary, held in the Western Reserve Historical Society, Cleveland, published as *With Sheridan Up the Shenandoah Valley* in 1864 (Cleveland and Dayton, 1989). *Mary Chestnut's Civil War*, C. Vann Woodward, ed. (New Haven, 1981), a new edition of that South Carolinian's valuable diary of the period, is rich in background and insight. The University of South Carolina Press is engaged in a project to publish less well-known diaries of southern women.

Victorian Ambitions

Brucemore is the only National Trust house that was built new during the High Victorian period. No historical research is yet available in print to document this fine Iowa mansion, although local history materials are useful. Helpful was Ralph Clements, *Tales of the Town: Little Known Anecdotes of Life in Cedar Rapids* (Cedar Rapids, 1967); *Glimpses of Cedar Rapids* by Charles B. Armstrong (Cedar Rapids, 1898) is filled with information on local businesses and businessmen like the Sinclairs. The architectural context is probably best found in Chicago's architectural history; see John Drury's chapter on the Queen Anne in his *Old Chicago Houses* (Chicago, 1941 and 1975) and pertinent chapters in David Lowe's *Lost Chicago* (Boston, 1975). Elizabeth Aslin's *The Aesthetic Movement* (New York, 1969), although concerned with English design, is still the best source on the Queen Anne in decorative arts.

Art Turns the Century

Books and articles abound on Frank Lloyd Wright, but one must begin with *An Autobiography* (New York, 1932, 1943). A classic on his work is Henry-Russell Hitchcock's *In the Nature of Materials* (New York, 1942 and 1973). The memoir written by the architect's son John Lloyd Wright, *My Father Who Is on Earth* (New York, 1946), recounts a childhood in the Oak Park home. Robert C. Twombly, *Frank Lloyd Wright: His Life and Architecture* (New York, 1979), concisely treats the early life and practice in Oak Park.

Chesterwood is an archive in itself, being almost exactly as Daniel Chester French left it. French's papers are being edited for publication by Michael Richman (forthcoming, University of California Press). Family albums chronicle daily life and amusements at Chesterwood. Mary French's *Memories of a Sculptor's Wife* (Boston, 1928) is a personal account, as is Margaret French Cresson's *Journey Into Fame: The Life of Daniel Chester French* (Cambridge, Mass., 1947). French's work is depicted in *Daniel Chester French: An American Sculptor* by Michael Richman (New York, 1976; Washington, 1983).

Paul Kester's papers are in the Museum of the City of New York. Some of Elizabeth Sharpe's are at Mount Vernon, but few others have been found.

America Joins the World

Filoli awaits a detailed history. The property has published a guide, "Filoli," compiled by Timmy Gallagher (San Francisco, 1990). Richard Longstreth, *On the Edge of the World: Four Architects in San Francisco at the Turn of the Century* (Cambridge, Mass., 1983), deals with the early practice of its architect, Willis Polk. A collection of Polk's papers is held by the College of Environmental Design, University of California, Berkeley; Bruce Porter's are in that university's Bancroft Library. William Bowers Bourn's life was very public and is easily traced in publications and journals of his day.

The Papers of Woodrow Wilson, Arthur S. Link, ed., have been published in sixty-three volumes (Princeton, 1966–1993). Edith Bolling Wilson's papers are in the Library of Congress; her *My Memoir* (Indianapolis, 1938) is revealing, but a far more engrossing book about Wilson House is Gene Smith, *When the Cheering Stopped* (New York, 1964).

A substantial group of William du Pont's business papers relating to Montpelier are at that site.

The Pope-Leighey House (Washington, 1969), the account of the National Trust's Usonian house, was edited by Terry B. Morton; it is a collection of dialogues with the client, builder, Wright's employees, and others connected with the construction and later relocation of the house. Some material comes from conversations with Marjorie Leighey in 1981 and 1982.

A Place for the Past

The historic preservation movement has its historian in Charles B. Hosmer, Jr., whose *Presence of the Past* (New York, 1965) traces preservation activities up to the early twentieth century; the subsequent account, *Preservation Comes of Age: From Williamsburg to the National Trust, 1926–1949,* 2 vols. (Charlottesville, 1981, for the National Trust for Historic Preservation) brings the story to the founding of the national preservation organization. *The History of the National Trust for Historic Preservation, 1963–1973* by Elizabeth D. Mulloy (Washington, 1976) covers the period during which many of the properties described here were acquired.

Houses of the National Trust for Historic Preservation

BELLE GROVE
1794

Striking in its pastoral setting of open land, Belle Grove stands near the eastern head of the valley of Virginia, its stone walls still bearing the marks of the original stonecutters. The tall interiors, almost unchanged since they were built for James Madison's sister and her husband, echo with memories of the wounded and dying during the Civil War battle that took place here.

Residents:
Nelly Madison and Isaac Hite
Ann Tunstall Maury Hite
Benjamin and John Cooley
General Philip H. Sheridan
Francis Welles Hunnewell

Belle Grove, Inc.
U.S. Route 11
Middletown, Virginia 22645
703-869-2028

Open mid-March to mid-November, 10:00 A.M. to 4:00 P.M.; Sunday, 1 P.M. to 5:00 P.M. Admission fee. Special event: Farm Craft Days, June

BRUCEMORE
1884–1886

This gabled Queen Anne mansion of red brick has been continually and lovingly maintained. The personalities of its occupants are projected in its interiors, from the dark, timbered stairhall to the sunny parlors and tin-roofed Tahitian room in the basement. Twenty-six acres of grounds abound in lawns and flowers.

Residents:
Caroline and Thomas Sinclair
Irene and George Bruce Douglas
Margaret Douglas and Howard Hall

Brucemore, Inc.
2160 Linden Drive, S.E.
Cedar Rapids, Iowa 52403
319-362-7375

Open February to December, Tuesday to Saturday, 10:00 A.M. to 3:00 P.M.; tours on the hour. Admission fee. Special events: Celebration of the Arts, Father's Day, June; Dixieland Jazz on the Green, mid-July Sunday; Victorian Christmas, Thanksgiving to Christmas

CASA AMESTI
c. 1834, 1846

A place that more completely recalls Mexican California than Polk Street in Monterey would be hard to find. Here two houses of the Vallejo sisters face each other in adobe splendor. Don Jose Amesti, a mayor of Monterey, built this house across the street from what is now the Cooper-Molera Adobe. Enlarged and now operated as a club, it reflects the time and 1920s taste of fashionable designer Frances Adler Elkins.

Residents:
Prudenciana Vallejo and
Don José Galo Amesti
The French Woman
Frances Adler and Felton Elkins

Old Capital Club
516 Polk Street
Monterey, California 93940
408-372-2311

Open Thursday to Tuesday, 10:00 A.M. to 4:00 P.M. (5:00 P.M. in the summer). Tours on the hour except 1:00 P.M. Admission fee. Special events: Annual Adobe Tour, April; Christmas in the Adobes, December

CHESTERWOOD
1898, 1901

The summer retreat of sculptor Daniel Chester French seems as though French, who died in 1931, has just stepped away. His studio, designed by Henry Bacon, survives intact, as does the family's Colonial Revival house. The garden retains its classic beauty, with an abundance of peonies and tall ferns. Part of the significant collection of sculpture by French is on view in the converted barn. Chesterwood is one of the few Berkshire estates open to the public.

Residents:
Mary and Daniel Chester French
Margaret French Cresson

4 Williamsville Road
P.O. Box 827
Stockbridge, Massachusetts 01262
413-298-3579

Open May 1 to October 31, 10:00 A.M. to 5:00 P.M. Admission fee. Special events: Antique Car Show, May; Contemporary Sculpture Show, July to October; Summer's Compliments Flower Show, July; Christmas at Chesterwood, November

CLIVEDEN
1763–1767

Battle-scarred from the Revolution, Cliveden was a family home for some two hundred years. It is filled with memorabilia of the Chew family and later generations. With its fine furniture, family portraits, and paintings, it is one of the greatest eighteenth-century houses in the Philadelphia area.

Residents:
Elizabeth Oswald and Benjamin Chew
Blair McClenachan
Katherine and Benjamin Chew, Jr.
Anne Sophia Penn Chew
Mary Johnson Brown and Samuel Chew
Bessie Chew
Samuel Chew III

Cliveden, Inc.
6401 Germantown Avenue
Philadelphia, Pennsylvania 19144
215-848-1777

Open Tuesday to Saturday, 10:00 A.M. to 4:00 P.M.; Sunday, 1 to 4 P.M.; closed January to March except by appointment. Admission fee. Special event: Commemoration of the Battle of Germantown, October

COOPER-MOLERA ADOBE
c. 1832

Across the street from Casa Amesti, this adobe built several years earlier by the Yankee seaman John Cooper and his Mexican wife is fully restored to show the Cooper family's long tenure. Its rooms now glow with remembrances of the last days of Mexico in California.

Residents:
Encarnacion Vallejo and
John Rogers Cooper
Rachel Holmes and Thomas Larkin
Frances Mary Molera

California Department
of Parks and Recreation
and Old Monterey Preservation Society
525 Polk Street
Monterey, California 93940
408-649-7118

Open Thursday to Sunday, 10:00 A.M. to 4:00 P.M. Admission fee. Special events: Annual Adobe Tour, April; Christmas in the Adobes, December

DECATUR HOUSE
1818–1819

Overlooking Lafayette Park, this is the capital's second most famous and romantic house. Designed by Benjamin H. Latrobe, Decatur House today shows several periods in its history, but it is Marie Beale's house most of all. California memorabilia of her swashbuckling father-in-law, Edward Beale, mingle with reminders of her life here.

Residents:
Susan and Stephen Decatur
Baronness and Baron Hyde de Neuville
Henry Clay
Martin Van Buren
Edward Livingston
Sir Charles Vaughn
John Gadsby
Natalie and Judah P. Benjamin
Mary and Edward Fitzgerald Beale
Marie and Truxtun Beale

748 Jackson Place, N.W.
Washington, D.C. 20006
202-842-0920

Open Tuesday to Friday, 10:00 A.M. to 2:00 P.M.; Saturday, Sunday, and holidays, 12:00 to 4:00 P.M. Special events: Architectural Quilts Show, January and February; Crafts Marketplace, November

DRAYTON HALL
c. 1738–1742

This magnificent Anglo-Palladian mansion surveys the Ashley River near Charleston, preserved as much for its poetry as for its architecture. Time has polished Drayton Hall to a high perfection of old age. It remained in the same family for nearly two and a half centuries and today evokes the memories of many generations, too beautiful as it is to restore to any conjectural vision of what it might have been.

Residents:
John Drayton
William Henry Drayton
Charles Henry Drayton
Dr. John Drayton
Charles Henry Drayton IV
Charlotta Drayton

3380 Ashley River Road
Charleston, South Carolina 29414
803-766-0188

Open daily, 10:00 A.M. to 4:00 P.M.; winter, 10:00 A.M. to 3:00 P.M. Admission fee. Student programs. Special events: Candlelight Concert, March; Oyster Roasts, March and April; Arts and Crafts Festival, Thanksgiving weekend; Spirituals Concert, December

FILOLI
1915–1917

With their colorful array of plantings and numerous carefully planned and pruned views of sky, Filoli's sixteen acres of gardens are among America's best. The work of landscape architect Bruce Porter and floral designer Isabella Worn, they seem all the more lush in their relatively dry countryside. The Georgian-style house was designed by Willis Polk.

Residents:
Agnes and William Bowers Bourn
Lurline and William Roth

Filoli Center
Canada Road
Woodside, California 94062
415-364-2880

Open mid-February to mid-November, Tuesday to Saturday; tours 10:00 A.M. and 1:00 P.M. Admission fee. Children under twelve years restricted to nature hikes. Special events: Jazz Concerts, May to September; Christmas at Filoli, November to December

FRANK LLOYD WRIGHT HOME AND STUDIO
1889–1898

In this residence and studio, from 1889 to 1909 Frank Lloyd Wright established himself and his personal style. The house borrows from the Shingle Style, but in the studio, added later to the side, Wright's distinctive mark is clear. The home and studio has been restored to the last year Wright spent here.

Residents:
Catherine Tobin and Frank Lloyd Wright
Catherine, David, Frances, John, Llewellyn, and Lloyd Wright

Frank Lloyd Wright Home and
Studio Foundation
951 Chicago Avenue
Oak Park, Illinois 60302
708-848-1976

Tours Monday to Friday, 11:00 A.M., 1:00 P.M., and 3:00 P.M.; weekends, 11:00 A.M. to 4:00 P.M. Admission fee. Special events: Walking Tours of the Prairie School Historic District; Wright Plus House Tour, May.

FRANK LLOYD WRIGHT'S POPE-LEIGHEY HOUSE
1939–1941

Houses were always a special interest of Frank Lloyd Wright, especially so in the depression days of the 1930s. This Usonian design represents his quest for quality housing at a reasonable cost. Saved from the path of a highway and moved from its original site, the small residence now is tucked into a portion of the National Trust property Woodlawn, where its wood-sheathed interior opens visually to the forest—providing a surprising contrast to the early nineteenth-century mansion.

Residents:
Charlotte and Loren Pope
Marjorie and Robert Leighey

U.S. Route 1
P.O. Box 37
Mount Vernon, Virginia 22121
703-780-4000

Open March to December, 9:30 A.M. to 4:30 P.M.; January and February, weekends only, 9:30 A.M. to 4:30 P.M. Special architectural and photographic tours. Admission fee.

LYNDHURST
1838, 1864–1865

Perched above the Hudson River, this Gothic confection from the hand of A. J. Davis sits amid sweeping lawns with fine old trees. Of its several owners, it survives chiefly as the home of Jay Gould, the misunderstood millionaire. His daughter Helen made it a shrine; her younger sister, Anna, returned here in old age to recall a happy childhood.

Residents:
William and Philip Paulding
Robert James Dillon
Julia and George Merritt
Helen and Jay Gould
Helen Gould and Finley J. Shepard
Anna Gould

635 South Broadway
Tarrytown, New York 10591
914-631-0046

Grounds open daily, 10:00 A.M. to 5:00 P.M.. House tours May to October, Tuesday to Sunday, 10:30 A.M. to 4:15 P.M.; November to April, weekends, 10:00 A.M. to 3:30 P.M. Special events: Antiques Show, April; Rose Day, June; Sunset Serenades, July; Candlelight Tours, December

MONTPELIER
c. 1755

Occupied continuously since the eighteenth century, Montpelier was established by the grandfather of James Madison. The president's father started the mansion, Madison expanded it, and it was enlarged in the twentieth century by William du Pont, whose family it served for two generations. The view of the Blue Ridge from Madison's front porch is one of the finest anywhere.

Residents:
Nelly and James Madison, Sr.
Dolley and James Madison, Jr.
Anna and William du Pont
Marion du Pont Scott

Route 20
P.O. Box 67
Montpelier Station, Virginia 22957
703-672-2728

Open 10:00 A.M. to 4:00 P.M. Admission fee. Special event: Montpelier Hunt Races, November

OATLANDS
c. 1804

George Carter's elegant neoclassical house is preserved as it was during most of this century, when the descendants of William Wilson Corcoran, the capital's great art patron, lived here in the summer and fall. Green pastures, terraced gardens, and an old greenhouse contribute to the completeness of this Virginia estate.

Residents:
Elizabeth and George Carter
Benjamin Carter
Kate and George Carter II
Edith and William Corcoran Eustis
Anne Eustis Emmet
Margaret Eustis Finley

Oatlands, Inc.
Route 15
P.O. Box 352
Leesburg, Virginia 22075
703-777-3174

Open April to December, Monday to Saturday, 10:00 A.M. to 4:30 P.M.; Sunday, 1:00 P.M. to 4:30 P.M. Admission fee. Special events: Sheep Dog Trials, May; Draft Horse and Mule Day, September; Garden Fair, September

SHADOWS-ON-THE-TECHE
1831–1834

No southern house calls up the romantic mood of the antebellum past like the Shadows, although its strongest voice came from its last owner, Weeks Hall. Built during boom years, when sugar was king, the house was home to Hall's great-grandparents. Time has melded it to its setting of great old trees and somber Spanish moss. To the rear the Bayou Teche recalls the days of steamboats, flatboats, and keelboats.

Residents:
Mary Clara and David Weeks
Judge John Moore
Weeks Hall

Main Street
P.O. Box 9703
New Iberia, Louisiana 70562
318-369-6446

Open 9:00 A.M. to 4:30 P.M. Admission fee. Special events: Terror on the Teche, October; Shadows Family Christmas and Merry Making at the Shadows, December

WOODLAWN
c. 1800–1805

The striking site, overlooking the Potomac River from afar, was George Washington's wedding present to Martha's granddaughter Nelly Custis and the president's nephew Lawrence Lewis. Nelly filled her lofty rooms with mementoes of Washington and the Revolution, and she welcomed Lafayette here.

Residents:
Eleanor Parke (Nelly) Custis and Lawrence Lewis
Jacob Troth
Rachel Lincoln and John Mason
Paul Kester
Elizabeth Sharpe
Bertha and Oscar Underwood

U.S. Route 1
P.O. Box 37
Mount Vernon, Virginia 22121
703-780-4000

Open 9:30 A.M. to 4:00 P.M. Admission fee. Special events: Annual Needlework Exhibition, March; Heritage Arts, Crafts, and Antiques Day, May; Rose Garden Tea, May; Quilt Exhibition, October; Christmas Performances, December

WOODROW WILSON HOUSE
1915

Woodrow Wilson and his second wife, Edith, moved to this Embassy Row home, designed by Waddy Wood, when his presidency ended in 1921. After Wilson's death in 1924, Edith lived on here until she died in 1961. The roomy interiors, crossed by abundant light, are filled with the reminders of a long and distinguished career concluded at the world's center stage. Few presidential houses contain such a remarkable collection of personal possessions.

Residents:
Henry Parker Fairbanks
Edith Bolling and Woodrow Wilson

2340 S Street, N.W.
Washington, D.C. 20008
202-673-4034

Open Tuesday to Sunday, 10:00 A.M. to 4:00 P.M. Admission fee. Special events: Spring Garden Party, May; Kalorama House and Embassy Tour, September; Armistice Day celebration, November

Index